POWER OF
EMPLOYEE
ENGAGEMENT

POWER OF EMPLOYEE ENGAGEMENT

Authored by

HEMANT AGARWAL

Penman Books

Office No. 303, Kumar House Building,
D Block, Central Market, Opp PVR Cinema,
Prashant Vihar, Delhi 110085, India
Website: www.penmanbooks.com
Email: publish@penmanbooks.com

First Published by Penman Books 2019
Copyright © Hemant Agarwal 2019
All Rights Reserved.

Title: Power of Employee Engagement
ISBN: 978-93-89024-19-7

Acknowledgment

My work on this book has been the effort of many. The book has taken a more longer time from what I expected initially. After daily traveling of 50Kms for office and being a father of two little champs, the only time I left to work on the book was morning 5 to 7 or either 11to 1 in the night. This is the time when my kids are still sleeping, but my passion for writing my first book is at a peak.

First and foremost, I would like to thank God Almighty for giving me the strength, knowledge, ability and opportunity to undertake the process of writing this book together, and I realized how true this gift of writing is for me. You have granted me the power to trust in my passion and go after my aspirations. Without the blessings of God, this achievement of book writing would not have been possible.

Words can not express how grateful I am to my mother and father for all of the sacrifices that you've made on my behalf. You have supported me emotionally and financially because of whom I have been able to achieve the things, I have always been inspired.

This book is dedicated to my kids, Darsh and Dishi, who are just about the best children a dad could hope for: happy, loving, and fun to be with.

I get immense support from all my family members in my ventures. I am thankful to my brothers, sisters, and all other loved ones for their indescribable contributions to my life. I consider myself the luckiest person in the world to have such a lovely and caring family, standing beside me all the times with their love and unconditional support.

To meet challenges of the corporate world, I have devoted lots of my personal time for learning new skills, techniques to keep pace with the world which could not have come through without sacrifices from my wife. She also provided motivation in writing a book, often by asking: When are you going to finish this..?

The World is an amazing place, thanks to people who want to develop and direct others. What makes it even better are people who share the gift of their time to mentor future leaders. In writing my book, I had to take the help and guidance of some respected persons who deserve my deepest gratitude. At the completion of this book gave me much pleasure, I would wish to express my gratitude to Dr. Virender Saroha (President – HR) for making me good guidelines for throughout numerous consultations.

Writing a book is harder than I thought and more rewarding than I could have ever imagined. I would like to thanks my colleagues in the office who stood by me during every struggle and all my successes. That's a true team where I enjoyed working.

Special thanks to Gourav Bhardwaj, Prem Chand, Rajesh Kaushik & Rahul Jayant for being part of life for 7+ years in Delhi NCR. Without their contribution to the professional and personal front, I may not gather enough courage to complete my first book in life. In their own ways, they kept me going on my path to success, assisting me as per their abilities, in whatever manner possible and for ensuring that good times keep flowing together.

Quick thanks to Sandeep for clicking & editing some of the beautiful pictures of mine required for the author page of the book.

Special appreciation for the publishing team of Penman for helping and guiding me throughout the book publication. Hats of to Tarun, you are a great guy... Keep the good work up..!!

I would also like to expand my gratitude to all those who have directly and indirectly guided me in writing my first book.

Preface

*"Your number one customer are your people.
Look after employees first and then customers last."*

—Ian Hutchinson, Author of People Glue

This quote beautifully described what I meant in this book. One fine day I am exploring some employee engagement activities for my organization, I don't find a single reference where I could refer various engagement programs which one can apply in the organization to improve engagement in one place, so is the book. It will help Leadership Team, Managers, line leaders, HR Members to be having information on various engagement programs they can apply in their organization.

I am not the author and not pretended to be the subject expert of Employee Engagement. I researched and brought up 151 activities to improve engagement levels of employees across all levels in the organization. Some of the activities can be implemented immediately and without incurring any cost or just negligible cost. You also might be doing some or many of the activities in your organization as well in the same or another manner.

Almost every employee engagement activity mentioned in the book might have already been said/ written by someone and implemented in many of the organizations. I don't claim to be the originator of these ideas, and I duly respect the rights of the ideas by the initiators. The activities mentioned in the book are gathered from different organizations after having one to one conversation with many HR Members, through various forums, books last but not the least research on the internet.

While I do not guarantee miracles to the organizations after reading and implementing activities that are willing to improve employee engagement as their workplace, in any case, I can surely ensure improved employee commitment in the organizations who apply a few or a large portion of the exercises and practices mentioned in the book.

First very important step all you have to do to understand your Top Management & Leadership Team about the importance of employee engagement in the organization. There are many advantages of employee engagement. I believe the most important one is engaging employee's retention percentages are remarkably higher than others.

Existing employee retention is critical for all organizations due to turn over expensive, and the top performers are always driving the business at all times in any organization. At the same point of time, it is equally important to make sure that the new employee should be enhanced and engaged as they can give fresh ideas and contribute to a new process, system, technology, etc. in the organization. Also, it's been essential to retaining new talents as they can also be a significant impact on the future of the organization.

Employees represent the brand, the image, and the core values of any organization irrespective of its size. In fact, employees are the face of the organization. These same employees are also responsible for carrying out the strategy and achieving the business results/objectives defined by Management & the leadership team from time to time.

It becomes easier if all employees are actively engaged, and all of that becomes a lot harder to accomplish when employees are disengaged, and the situation worsens when the employees are highly disengaged.

So we pose the question? How valuable is it to ensure employees are engaged?

Quite a number of studies state that employee engagement is the psychological connection that an employee feels for their organization, and such a relationship directly influences them to exert some discretionary effort to their work. If this is so, then employee engagement should be considered a competitive advantage for any company or business enterprise irrespective of its size.

Engagement in the organization is the emotional commitment an employee has to their organization and its goals. Engaged employees aren't just working for a salary paycheck in the month-end; instead, they genuinely care about their organization's mission, vision, and goals.

This discretionary effort makes employees go far and beyond their call of duty; it keeps them committed in good and bad times and also a part of a winning climate, and much more.

Do not assume that because the employment market is so bad, your employees definitely have no other place to go, so you are at rest and not bothered."

Employee retention is not synonymous with employee engagement; it is not getting the best performance from your

staff. Irrespective of your retention rate, employees can still have low engagement, which directly impacts performance and dedication, both collectively and individually.

You might be thinking – they have nowhere to go, and so they are so thankful to you for just having a job and that this is sufficient. Oh, you are making a huge mistake, and in case you haven't thought of it already, I can assure you, there are plenty opportunities for them to explore out there and once they discover that the coast is clear, they take their leave.

Engagement impacts commitment and performance both now and later. It takes decent some time and effort to build and improve employee engagement. It's high time you start working on it right away.

You can measure your employee's engagement with a survey, today, analyze the information collected and develop an action strategy to boost engagement.

Your employees have more than enough competencies and potentials to take your company to the next level. They possess great ideas on how to boost your company's productivity, growth and gain, quality, customer service, customer satisfaction, customer loyalty, and what could be done in order to boost your risk profile.

It's quite essential for you to understand how satisfied or dissatisfied your employees are while working at your organization. Endeavor to know how engaged they can be and what can be done in order to increase their level of engagement.

While most companies know the importance of taking actions and creating improvements to be competitive, they often miss significant hidden actions that can definitely make a difference to customers, employees, and the bottom line.

This BOOK offers the best, most cost-effective way about what needs to be done to increase employee satisfaction and engagement in the organization. The book is equally useful for HR Managers, Business Leaders, Managers, Line Leaders, Business Heads, Plants Heads, Corporate Heads, CEO, MD, Top Management and also students who want to pursue their projects in Employee Engagement.

Remember, highly satisfied employees get more engaged in their jobs, their productivity is higher, and they do more to generate profit for your business.

"POWER OF EMPLOYEE ENGAGEMENT" is the quintessential increasing employee engagement and improving employee satisfaction with proven strategies that apply to any industry. **The book offers 151 Employee Engagement Practices and activities that an organization needs to improve employee satisfaction and engagement.**

If you want to ensure you increase employee engagement and create an environment in which everyone from upper management to entry-level employees feels respected and as if they're part of a winning team, start reading now and I hope you will make the best use of it.

Happy Reading..!!

Contents

CHAPTER
One

Introduction to
Employee Engagement

There's a lot of disagreements about what employee engagement is all about. Various research works define employee engagement in different ways.

Being a vast subject, employee engagement cannot have a single definition. Different organizations define employee engagement in a different way.

Some equate engagement with job satisfaction, others talk about emotional commitment to a person's work and organizations, others use the notion of 'discretionary effort' as an indication that a person is engaged and some relate with employee retention in the organization.

Engaged organizations attract talent, retain top performers, and drive results. Positive employee recognition makes every employee feel appreciated, and that leads to better results for your company in the long run.

There is no globally agreed definition of engagement amongst the consultants and experts. Here's a selection that represents the most common definitions

1. **Engagement represents the energy, effort, and initiative employees bring to their jobs' (Harvard Business Review)**

2. **The psychology of how each employee connects with customers and with the organization'** (Gallup)

3. **Staff commitment and a sense of belonging to the organization.' (Hewitt)**

4. **Employees' commitment to the organization and motivation to contribute to the organization's success.' (Mercer)**

5. **Employees' exertion of "discretionary effort"... going beyond meeting the minimum standards of the job.'**

The term 'employee engagement' is a relatively new one and as well as being described by some as the latest HR fraternity it is muddled and confusing area because of the lack of clarity of definition.

There's no wonder that those who are supposed to be responsible for employee engagement often struggle to work out what their job is about to let alone what they are supposed to achieve.

The fact is that it is a very complex area because so many different variables determine whether or not someone is engaged. Those variables include factors external to the person, e.g., their manager, the culture of the organization, the pay, and the reward system.

They also include internal factors, including the person's personality type, their values, and the meaning they make from their own work.

An organization's employees are said to be engaged when employees at all levels of the company are fully committed, devoted and dedicated to their jobs and their company

- Engaged employees are always able, willing, and ready to do anything in their capacity to contribute to their organization's success.

- Engaged employees can go the extra mile for their organization, by so imputing effort in their work far and beyond expectation. They are always willing and eager to work extra hours thus focusing their inspiration, experience, energy, and abilities to be successful for themselves and the company they work with

- Engaged employees do thrive excellently when they work in a positive corporate culture. Their power, inspiration, and excitement, in turn, go a long way in boosting the corporate culture.

For an organization to achieve sustainable growth, among the fundamentals that have to be embraced is that of maintaining and keeping talent for every crucial single role defined within the organization. For many years now, employee engagement has been a common issue in the corporate world.

Employee engagement has attracted the attention of Human resource managers, business gurus, as well as research organizations. The basic idea is that when employees are fully engaged, they will be motivated to act in ways that promote their company interests, and they won't have any reason to leave their jobs for alternatives.

Among the hallmarks of good organization, management is to know how to attract and keep talents. The typical method of using sticks and carrot to keep their employees engaged is a widely used approach, but it is only a partial step.

Such extrinsic and intrinsic rewards send messages to employees about what behavior is appreciated, and what type of climate the company wishes to create for its employees.

Undoubtedly, dissatisfaction among employees may result in absenteeism, high turnover, and lots more, all of which can be detrimental to organizational sound performance.

Now the question is when engagement begins – Nevertheless Engagement must begin at the commencement of the employee lifecycle in the organization, right from recruitment, and continues through onboarding, induction, career planning, learning and development, leadership and succession planning, and retirement of the employee or exit from the organization.

Factors for Higher Employee Engagement

Here is a list of some very important and vital factors contributing to higher employee engagement in any organization:

- Understanding of corporate Goals/ Mission/ Vision
- Understanding of job and how it contributes to overall corporate goals
- Clear communication of goals, expectations, directions
- Job design
- & Job fit
- Support and tools
- Independence & innovation
- Relationship with boss/direct reports
- Clear feedback on performance
- Recognition
- Learning and development opportunities
- Pride in organization
- Employee involvement in decision making
- Work-life balance
- Workplace culture/morale
- Co-worker relationships/good team environment (enjoy colleagues)
- Fair HR practices
- Empowerment
- Encouragement

Employee engagement doesn't mean...

.... Employee satisfaction. A satisfied employee might show up to his/her workplace daily 9 to 5:30 or so without failure. But that same "satisfied" employee might not go the extra mile to make an effort, and will probably take a call to go away with a 10% jump in pay. Satisfied isn't enough.

.... Employee happiness. An employee might be happy at work, but that doesn't necessarily mean that they are working hard, productive, making extra efforts on behalf of the organization. While company luring add-ons such as game rooms, training, vacations, fun and parties, recognitions & skills development may be sweet and attractive for various reasons, it actually makes employees happy which is different from keeping them engaged in the organization.

CHAPTER
Two

Classification of Employees

Depending on the amount of employees commitment in the organization, the employees can be classified into three categories:

1. Engaged Employees

2. Not Engaged

3. Actively Disengaged

Engaged Employees

This is the first category of employees in the organization and is those who can be seen working in the organization with passion, alignment, commitment, and innovation; which means that they are passionate, connected to the company, committed to timely completion of tasks assigned to him/her and are innovative as one of their core competencies .

These employees contribute new ideas and turn ideas into reality. These employees are optimistic in their viewpoint, and they extend positivity. They are proactive; can anticipate future market conditions are prepared well in advance.

They individualize the company's goals and objectives and perpetually work on top of and on the far side of their job necessities for the betterment of the organization. These types of employees are real victors in the organization.

Not Engaged

This is the second category of employees in the organization and found to be in large numbers which are almost 50% of total employees in the organization (as per the various surveys held from time to time). These categories of employees need to be guided for taking work from them, and they do what is told only by their supervisors and managers, and they like only one instruction at a time. They put their time in completing the tasks assigned to them but not with the same level of energy and passion which engaged employee possesses.

These employees may be either positive or negative in their outlook and perception about the organization depending on the prevailing atmosphere in the organization. These types of employees are not proactive and sometimes fail to anticipate the requirement of coming future and not actively ready for technological advancements. They work what is desired by their supervisors and managers.

These staff will hold either a negative or positive perspective towards the organization. They contemplate their job as a payroll check, nothing a lot of.

Actively Disengaged Employees

This is the third category of employees in the organization who are unhappy with un-obvious regions, and at the same time, they spread unhappiness in the organization too. These categories of employees are harmful to any organization in both environments - internally and externally. These employees are sad, resentful, and unfold negativity at intervals of the organization. They are observed to disease centers in the organization as they spread the negative word about the organization as well as organizational employees.

Provoking, and convincing employees to leave their jobs are their prime aim.

CHAPTER
Three

Pillars of Employee Engagement

Based on interactions with different organizations and employees, **I have arrived on nine pillars of employee engagement** in which we can categorize employee engagement programs & activities in the organization:

1. **Rewards & recognition:** Their organization appreciates the good work done by the employees. Rewards & recognition is an encouraging and motivating factor for any employee.

2. **Growth:** The ultimate goal is to make sure that employee growth is well taken care of in the organization, along with an ideal amount of both engagement and satisfaction.

3. **Health & Wellness:** Employees with strong and effective physical and mental wellness programs in place. This is the most crucial part as healthy and fit employees are more productive in the organization.

4. **Alignment:** When it comes to alignment of employees with the organization, it requires a top-down approach. The best part is aligned organizations are very responsive to changes and at the same time taking their employees along. Alignment is essential to sustain a high-performance culture.

5. **Collaboration:** Employees want to experience the connection that comes from doing good work with good people at any level, directly or indirectly.

6. **Motivation/Encouragement:** Employees want to experience a sense that their work matters in the organization. As an employer, organizations want to have their people motivated and encouraged. When employees have motivation at work, they will inspire them to do good work and find ways to complete their tasks in a faster way.

7. **Happiness:** Happiness is a state observed by employees while doing their work in the organization and to the extent to which employees feel good about their jobs. Happiness is the most vital factor of engagement in the workplace.

8. **Acceptance:** It refers to how organization values and needs the ideas and experience of their employees in the organization. More accepted employees are, the most engaged organization will become.

9. **Knowledge & Skills:** The focus of organizations towards developing the knowledge and skills of the employee both personal skills as well as skills required for performing their jobs.

CHAPTER
Four

The Rising Importance of Employee Engagement

A fully engaged employee is emotionally and intellectually bound to the organization, gives 100 percent, feels passionate about its goals, and is committed to living by its values. These engaged employees go beyond the basic job responsibility to delight the customers and drive the business forward. Moreover, in times of diminishing loyalty, employee engagement is a powerful tool for retention strategy for any organization.

Various research shows that engaged employees possess to:

1. Perform better in their work areas

2. Put in extra efforts whenever required to help get the job done in a timely manner

3. Shows a very high level of commitment to the organization

4. Highly motivated and optimistic about his/her goals of the work area and the organization.

5. Actively takes the lead forward without their supervisor/manager tells about work

Organizations with engaged employees tend to experience low employee turnover and more impressive business outcomes.

Engaged employees are committed, motivated, and emotionally connected to the company. Actively disengaged employees don't care about the company.

Successful employee engagement creates a better system & processes, positive work culture, and enables better management in the organization, so employees are happier and more productive at work. This ultimately leads to better employee morale, more satisfied customers, higher quality products, less attrition rate, and higher profits for organizations. Some of the benefits of employee engagement program are mentioned herewith:

- **Increased Employee Satisfaction**
  - Surveys revealed that actively engaged organizations tend to have a higher satisfaction level in the organization compared to disengaged employees. Solicitously implemented engagement programs/activities bring multiple benefits to employees at all levels. Training & developmental Activities, career planning, health & wellness programs, different employee benefit schemes, etc. are proven to bring more satisfaction to the employees irrespective of their level in the organizational hierarchy. Satisfied employees are the backbones of any organization.

- **Better Employee Health**
  - Mental & physical health has begun to become a commonplace problem among employees

around the world. These issues can occur as anxiety, panic, or depression, or it just could be experienced as stress and burnout. Engaged employees found to have better health (both Mental& Physical).

- **Improved Employee Loyalty**
  - According to various research conducted from time to time, organizations whose employees are more engaged at work tends to show superior loyalty than the disengaged employees in the organization.

- **Less absenteeism**
  - An engaged employee is more committed to the timeliness of work and possesses less absenteeism in comparison to disengaged employees. The engaged employee takes leave and gets off from work when it's extremely necessary & unavoidable.

- **Increase in Customer Satisfaction**
  - A satisfied and engaged employee will go the extra mile to make their customers happy and plays an important & vital role in keeping the customers pleased with the product and services of the organization. According to a study done by Hay Group, engaged employees help the organization grow in revenue twice as

much as those with lower engagement levels. Everyone is dedicated to meeting the needs and expectations of the customer in any way they can.

- **Improved Organization's reputation**

  - An engaged employee takes care of the brand in the market. It also acts as a tool for internal branding and sometimes off chances, external of the organization.

- **Higher Innovation**

  - Not only employees do need to understand why innovation is critical to the organization, but they also truly understand how the work they do makes into the overall efforts of the organization.

- **Better Sales & Growth**

  - Employee engagement is one of the critical tools in employee retention and maintaining the productivity of the organization resulting in better sales and margins.

- **Low Attrition rate**

  - Employee engagement leads to commitment and psychological attachment of the employees to the organization and replicates in the form of improved retention of the employees. If your company promotes a culture whereby employees feel they are listened to, understood, and cared about, they will want to stay in the company and will not seek employment elsewhere.

- **Ownership**
  - Engaged employees carry on as though they were the proprietor of the association, advancing a similar exertion and responsibility that somebody who claims the business would do in each situation.

- **Healthy Company Culture**
  - A healthy culture at work can not only carry an amazing innovation and productivity but also improve employee motivation and engagement towards the organization.

- **Improved connectivity**
  - Employees who feel connected to their Managers will feel more comfortable in their sharing concerns and problems. The employee shall professionally and emotionally be attached to the organization. The more you learn about and take an interest in an employee's life, the more he or she will feel respected by you. This will result in the improved connection of the employee with the organization.

Why Engage..??

- Linkage with business results

  - **Hewitt Study:** High positive correlation between engagement scores & Total Shareholder Return/ sales growth

  - **Towers Perrin Study:** 17% higher operating margins

  - **Mercer Study:** Increase in employee engagement reduced employee turnover by 3% and resulted in an ROI of $3 million

  - **Great Places To Work Institute & Russell Investment Group:** Stock market performance of the best employers in the US outperforms major stock indices

CHAPTER
Five

*Prerequisites to Effective
Employee Engagement*

To define better employee engagement activities, one needs thoughtfully work on the prerequisites of the employee engagement programs. The major factors which need to be taken care of before planning the employee engagement programs in an organization are as follows:

1. Demography of workforce

2. Education Level

3. Type of work they are doing

4. Organization Culture

5. Working environment

6. Business Plan

7. Volume of workforce

8. Mission & Vision of the organization

9. Management Priorities

10. Size & capacity of the organization

Since Engagement programs vary from industry to industry, Engagement activities can be planned as per the above factors. The word "employee engagement" alone doesn't give you anything you can visualize. Try experimenting what it means for your employees of the organization to be explicitly engaged. Once you identify what employee engagement programs work in your company, you can set your visions on achieving it. One thing needs to be noted here; employee engagement cannot be achieved overnight.

Employee Engagement Activities differ from domain to domain, company to company, which is really important before arriving at the list of programs based on the focus areas of the organization. These focus areas could range from communication, management approachability, grievance handling, transparency & culture, Growth opportunities, Reward & Recognition, policies, Work-life balance, Business Plan, etc.

Employee Engagement practices must commence from the recruitment and selection stage, moving down to the induction and orientation process.

Be aware of cultural differences - With the growing levels of diversity, especially cultural diversity occurring in most of the organizations, it is very crucial for managers & supervisors to raise the issue of cultural differences in fun and humor. What seems appropriate for one group of people may not be well received by another.

The Difference Between Employee Satisfaction, Efficiency and Engagement

In an upward progression, satisfaction, efficiency and Engagement are all interrelated. Each product has distinct drivers, but to boost efficiency in the workplace, they build on each other.

Just because employees are happy & satisfied with their work does not imply that they are efficient or engaged with the organization. An employee can be fully satisfied with his or her work and not be fully engaged. An employee can be happy and efficient, but not engaged, to further complicate matters.

All components work together to create an environment where employees are highly motivated and committed to giving their best performance in the organization they work for.

CHAPTER
Six

Approaches to Employee Engagement

"Connect the dots between individual roles and the goals of the organization. When people see that connection, they get a lot of energy out of work. They feel the importance, dignity, and meaning in their job."

—Ken Blanchard

To help employee engagement, you need to understand what it really is? Employee engagement is the mechanism that you must take into consideration into any organization, either small or big. It doesn't mean employee happiness only. It is actually the level of enthusiasm and dedication an employee feels toward his or her job in the organization. It is the key to activating a high performing workplace.

Each employee needs a stress buster. Employees will value that you thought of them, employees will be able to convey what needs be more, and it'll cost your company next to negligible in the long run. At a higher level, they need to see development occurring and that the company keeps up a solid position in the market. Your employees are a lot more than employees and perceiving that will go an incredibly long way. When they feel that exhibition assessment is reasonable in the organization and there is no shrouded plan yet a distinct message, they will, in general, accept the leadership team and trust them better.

Your employees comprise more than their achievements at work. A few employees like to get celebrated openly. Empowered employees feel as if they have the right set of resources and tools to get the work assignment done without any hassles.

Basically, accept the open the door to grasp how your employees like to get perceived. Support the way of life of collaboration inside your organization and consider the employees perform far superior what they can actually do. To succeed in their jobs, they need to understand how they fit into the organization. At the opposite end of the cart are the employees who are neither engaged nor committed.

The important approached while planning & executing employee engagements programs are given here:

1. **Top to bottom approach**

    Employee engagement is such that it requires to be led by example. Until the top management doesn't believe in it and encourage their managers and further to their employees, it will not get absorbed into the culture of the organization.

2. **In line with Company Culture**

    Engagement must be in line with the company culture and values. Different employees tend to have a different capacity for engagement.

3. **Choose an engagement program carefully**

    Engagement for 20 years is different for engagement for 58 years older people. A 58-year employee might not be interested in learning PowerPoint presentations, and a 20-year-old employee will not show any interest in a coaching session on retirement planning.

4. **Communicate the vision, mission & future plans**

    Communicate the vision, mission & future plans of the organization in an inspiring way

    Make employees believe they are valued by heart - such employees provide ideas, work harder, serve customers, and relate better to customers. A focus on the intrinsic factors results in engaging employees with deep commitment.

5. **Take phase by phase approach**

    Plan your employee engagement program in phases so as not to create a mash-up of different engagement programs.

6. **Try and try until it works.**

    Keep on trying different approached of employee engagement until it works for you. Remember there is never an end of the road, so keep trying.

7. **Take feedback**

    Take feedback on regular intervals to access the appropriateness of engagement programs in the organization.

8. Expert Advice

Depending upon the size of Employee Engagement activities can be planned, there is no harm in getting a bit of expert advice from the consultants who have decades of experience in the field.

CHAPTER
Seven

Ownership of Employee Engagement

The responsibility of planning employee engagement activities and executing them in an organization is not an HR alone anymore. HR is not only responsible for engagement; in fact, Top Management, Leadership Team, Line Managers, and moreover employee himself is responsible for the success or failure of employee engagement. Its employee who needs to take a step forward and support engagement activities as it will be ultimately directly or indirectly beneficial for them only.

HR plays an important and vital role in executing employee engagement strategies, but the planning and execution require involvement from Top leaders, CXO's, managers, and supervisors in the organization as well. The effectiveness & success of an employee engagement program depends on employees' receptivity to it also. Employee engagement is an organization-wide collaborative function that requires active participation and cooperation at all levels in the organization.

It's very important that the responsibilities for each of engagement programs & activities must also be appropriately assigned to the engagement drivers and tracked to ensure the effectiveness of the engagement tools. Many time engagement initiatives fail not because they are not well planned and strategized, but because they are unsystematically executed.

Here the role of engagement leader plays an important & vital role in the success of engagement programs carried out in the organization. Now the question arises here, what makes a person engaging leader..?

On a broader parameter, the following are the qualities of a good engaging leader:-

- Passionate
- Inclusive
- Good Listener
- Inspiring
- Strong Values
- Visionaries
- Caring
- Humble
- Brave
- Acceptive
- Good Leader
- Decision Making

Ways to Keep Top Management Involved in Employee Engagement

1. It's very important to involve the Top leaders as well as HR involved in framing the employee

engagement programs/ activities. The only one does not drive engagement alone, HR, along with top leaders, needs to take way forward for implementing employee engagement programs in the organization.

2. Have top managers involved in the planning and directing of employee engagement initiatives by serving as chairpersons of these programs or serving on steering committees directing these initiatives.

3. Ask top managers for their input and suggestions about how these programs could be more successful in the organization.

4. Ask top managers for ideas and suggestions for projects to support employee engagement.

5. Ask top management to support training and awareness programs that are essential for employee engagement. Even employee training also improves behavioral, temperamental, emotional and mental attributes of their character, which is very critical for any organization. Support for the training budget would be a phenomenal step by the management.

6. Report progress and successes of employee engagement programs to top management on a regular basis. Include these reports in monthly or quarterly reports sent to top management.

7. Publicize top management's interaction and involvement in employee engagement programs.

8. Ask top management to present formal recognition awards to employees for significant accomplishments achieved as a result of engagement activities.

9. Invite top managers to attend meetings or other events related to employee engagement activities to gain a better understanding of what's involved in the process and the commitment level of employees.

10. Look for projects that top management could personally be more involved in either in a leadership capacity or even as a contributing member of a project team.

11. Identify savings or cost reductions that can be attributed to employee engagement and ensure that top management is aware of this financial impact of these initiatives.

CHAPTER *Eight*

Practices for Implementing Employee Engagement

While employee engagement does not transcend to greater productivity, it is definitely one of the essential factors for organizational success. The employees who are highly engaged are excited and enthusiastic about the company goals and objectives and are fully eager to contribute their own quota to their team's success.

This poses another question: Just how can you encourage involvement in the first place? Engagement is driven by quite a number of factors interrelated. I have compiled on my list top 151 best practices which are most critical to optimizing your organization employee engagement:

There are many ways to achieve this, beginning with a willingness to offer any training necessary to assist your employees to best fit in their current role, far and above what they want just to be happy with, their proficiency.

Another important way to help employees be engaged in their work is to help them understand the meaning underlying their work. Why does what they do matter? How does it help others or a cause? Employees want to know that they are making a difference and when they can see that, they feel more engaged.

Here at the end of this chapter, you will find:

- Cost-effective ways of encouraging positive interaction

- Tips to improve morale

- Strategies to not only help your employees work smarter but to make them care about their work and the organization as a whole

- Ways to improve their health and lower their stress levels via holistic approaches like yoga and meditation

- Tips to incentivize their accomplishments with rewards and employee recognition

- Ways to offer unlimited medical leaves to help ease employees mind

- And so much more!

So, here follows the 151 employee engagement activities & ideas that's works for engaging the workforce which anyone can start implementing in their organization.

8.1 Rewards & Recognition

*"Everyone wants to be appreciated,
so if you appreciate someone, don't keep it a secret."*

—Mary Kay Ash

1. Best Student Award

While going through research on Employee engagement activities, I came across to know one of the organizations; which gives the Best Student award to the children of the employees every year on the occasion of New year celebration who have attained good marks in their academics.

Also recognizing the children of Operator-level employees who are doing professional courses like MBA, B. Tech, M. Tech, C. A, MBBS, etc. Awarded children are called on the occasion of celebration in the organization along with his/her father/mother working in the organization. This will improve levels of belongings and respect in the employees as well as in their family members.

2. Best Workstation Award

Best workstation Award serves as an excellent tool to keep the organization clean and healthy by spreading competition among the individual/ teams to follow their workstation clean and organized. This activity can be held quarterly or half-yearly depending upon the size of the organization, and Movie Vouchers, Dinner Vouchers along with running trophy can be an added advantage. Running trophy will be kept by winning team/individual for the quarter on their workstation.

3. Long Service Award

Years of service awards programs are thus designed for the purposes of rewarding employees because of landmark accomplishments while working in the same company. Such concepts need execution through a well thought out plan. When this happens, such awards go a long way in galvanizing employees and in creating a workplace environment that is convivial and productive.

Long Service Awards are given to employees in recognition of their long service period with the company, the loyalty they have demonstrated, the commitment they have made, and in celebration of their having achieved significant career milestones. Long Service Award recognizes Employees who have completed 5 Years, 10 Years, 15 Years, 20 years, 25 years, and so on...... in the continuous Services of the organization. To make the occasion more memorable, a token of appreciation in the form of a certificate/memento and small gift to the employee will be noteworthy.

When someone finds an enjoyable job with a company that appreciates him or her, they tend to stay longer with that employer as much as possible — having a unique token to mark the anniversary of this bonding and boost their overall morale. Marking milestone years shows that the organization values loyalty and dedicated service.

4. Rewards & recognition

To reduce attrition rates, improve employee loyalty, attraction, and retention of outstanding staff, induce positive and constructive work environments; Rewards & recognition play an important & vital role in the organization. Rewards are given to recognize the specific/ unique value-added and critical performance incidents within or beyond expected & predefined performance objectives. To reward these performance incidents in monetary or non-monetary terms, indicating organizational recognition and appreciation towards the employees can be done in several ways. Example of some of the reward strategies are given here as under:-

Star Performance Award

This award is given to the employees for their outstanding contribution in their respective work areas by implementing innovative work practices, thereby giving a performance which exceeds the managers/ management expectation.

Employee of The Month/Quarter/Year

This award is given to the employees who have done outstanding work by saving the company money, improving product quality, increasing sales, help in the growth of the organization, discharging his/her responsibilities diligently by acting as an effective team player.

Team of The Year Award

This is a team-based award and given to Functional Team/Cross-Functional Team based on issues resolved, project handled, efficient dealing with customers, support provided or any such incidents/behaviors bringing insignificant impact on a customer's perception and Company's image building or done some outstanding work by saving company money, improving product quality, increasing sales/productivity, initiated some processes, help in the growth of the organization and troubleshooting.

Honesty Act of The Year Award

Honesty act of the year award is given to the person who demonstrates an outstanding act of honesty in the organization.

Project Completion Award

On completion of a specific project, which required more efficient and effective than the regular projects, this award is being given.

Exemplary Task Award

Exemplary Task award is being given to the employees who demonstrate an outstanding act, e.g., an act of bravery, sacrifice, fire fighting, etc. to set an example for others.

Customer Appreciated Performance Award

This award is given to the employees based on the customer feedback on issues resolved, comfort level with customers, the support provided or any such incidents/behaviors are bringing in a significant impact on a customer's perception and company's brand building.

Outstanding Innovation

This award is given to the employees for finding out a creative and innovative way to make some significant improvements in Quality of products & Service or making some cost-saving initiatives.

LEADERSHIP AND MANAGEMENT AWARDS

Department Heads, Sr. Team Leader, Business Heads, Corporate Heads, Regional Managers, General Managers, etc. who have shown exemplary leadership, have met significant goals, or have served tirelessly to meet a company initiative. These individuals have displayed amazing leadership skills and guided their teams. These are the people that should be recognized for their efforts.

5. Take an extra mile

Not to forget to do something special for employees when they take on extra pieces of work in addition to their own work profile while another employee is on vacation or out sick/on medical leave.

This well helps the managers & concerned team members to take the lead forward and take additional work in the absence of their team members and thus helping the organization by not leave any work dependencies.

6. Fair Performance Review and Compensation

Your employees are very important to your business & organization. You cannot accomplish different processes of the business without their contribution. Employees are the pillars of organizational growth and prosperity. Employees must be accountable for reaching goals through a structured performance review process.

Treating employees right and by giving them what they deserve in the organization are just some of the ways to show them they and integral & important part of the organization.

Fair Performance review of the appraisal year at par with Market standards plays an important & vital role. If any employee is less paid as per the market standards, the relevant salary Correction to be provided in accordance with the performance of the employee during the Appraisal Year. It will directly help in retaining the employee also boost his motivation.

7. Spot awards

Why wait long for yearly or quarterly or monthly occasions to award an employee for his/her excellent work, Spot Awards works as a motivational factor to performing employees to boost their morale in front of everybody. It also provides encouragement to other employees as well.

8. Quote for the day

This activity can be done by department wise. Anyone employee from each department should write a quote on their whiteboard. The HR Department should decide the best quote for the day from the quotes written by different departments on the notice board.

The department that gets the highest accredited points for the month would be offered a gift voucher for Dinner, Movie, Shopping for the team members of the department.

The activity aimed to encourage the employees to show their creativity and skills in writing the quotes.

9. Recognize the entire family

Recognition of employees is indeed it's great, but recognizing family serves as an outstanding step towards the engaged workforce. Involvement of an employee's family, so as to bring a sense of belongingness not only among employees but also among their family members.

10. Celebrate Success

Celebrate successes, whether it is big or small, make the workplace fun & encouraging. Sharing small-small successes & achievements with your Employees' in the organization is an excellent way of making the workplace fun & encouraging, not only by champagne, a two or more kilo of Ice Cream or a small cake or sandwiches with a 2 Liter of Cold Drink is good enough for the team, but you have to do what works best for you and organization.

It will warm you and the employees up and sets the celebration tone or if possible, celebrate positive momentum for some time by tapping out as affirmation as a way of expressing enhanced gratitude.

11. Reward Your Employees With Personalized Items

Personalized items reflect attention to detail. These details help to establish a feeling of individuality even if you are one of many. This holds particularly true in large organizations where there are thousands of other employees.

Even though employees may not be centrally located in one place, it bears remembering that they all work in one place. For some employees, their identity is something they don't want to lose even at work.

Personalized items that are presented to employees as rewards and incentives are a great way to recognize the individual in each employee. Whether your company wants to provide incentives and awards such as personalize laptop bags, briefcases, wall clocks, wristwatches, or some other item that serves a useful purpose. Adding the personalization to these items makes all the difference in the world.

12. Diversify Your Rewards Scheme

Rewards are a motivational factor to employees of any level in the organization. Don't consider giving your employees the same set of perks and rewards over and over again for the excellent work done. It can be one of the drivers behind the disappointment of an employee engagement program and causes of dis-engaged employees in the organization. If possible, give your employees the opportunity to pick their own rewards and recognition programs.

13. The reward for A Job Well Done

Rewarding and recognizing employees for a job well completed or executed them do have a great impact on employee engagement and retention. Smart and effective leaders understand what their folks do well and will ultimately reward them for work well done.

This kind of encouragement helps employees today achieve greater things exceeding their day-to-day endurance and comfort. It is a very important part of employee engagement to reward and recognize the individuals for their achievements in simple yet powerful ways. Lack of reward will definitely lead to the failure of the employee engagement plan.

14. Profit-Sharing

Start a profit-sharing or bonus program for the employees. In this plan, employees receive the percentage of profits based on the earnings of the company. It can be paid on a yearly basis after completion of the financial year or after preparing the balance sheet of the company. It will directly link the profits of the company with the productivity of the employees.

8.2 Growth

1. Career Growth

Show a well-defined growth path to your employees. It not only increases their motivation but also improves their loyalty towards the organization. If you can show your employee how he will grow with the growth of your company, he starts giving his 100% of the work. Else, if an employee believes that only your growth will take place due to work, he is doing. ***Neither the employee will be loyal to the organization, nor might he not give his 100% efficiency.*** Anytime, if someone pays him more than what you are paying, he will be going to leave your job.

2. Always provide learning opportunities and Career development

Millennials and Fast Trackers want to move fast and expect to be learning new things all the time. This expectation needs to be managed, as most organizations can't promote unless there are new roles or bigger or expanded roles. If millennials don't see room for growing their careers in the organization, they are going to move on.

3. Allow lateral movement within the organization

There are times in the organization when some employees (especially the younger ones) are still figuring out their career paths. On the off chance that a team member finds something different at your organization that they're enthusiastic about and need to seek after, make a guide to get them thereby extending the fullest cooperation. This will certainly help you retain some of your young talents when they might have otherwise abandoned ship.

4. Nurture a Growth Mindset

Employees with a growth mindset believe their abilities can be developed through dedication and hard work. They view their innate skills as a starting point and have a love for learning. Active feedback cultures value this mindset. They value learning and development. They see feedback as a good opportunity to improve. And they don't just say they value these things; they show it and integrate it into their business.

5. Delegation

Delegation is beneficial for you since it extends your administrative range of control. It's useful for your employees since it is a development open door for them. It exhibits your trust in them to carry out the responsibility accurately and builds their responsibility for an errand.

Delegation can be started from small-small tasks before going for delegation bigger responsibilities.

6. Fast Trackers

The fast Trackers program's objective is to build a strong and young leadership pipeline at the middle management level in the organization. The program includes identifying high potential candidates, "FAST TRACKERS" in the organization and developing them for future critical roles, in line with the mission & vision for the next 2 years or 3 years or 5 years and beyond.

The selection process for Fast Trackers employees includes a review of the previous 2-3 years' performance, recommendation from the business leaders, review of assessment center scores by a cross-functional group before the decision is taken by the Committee.

Throughout the program, the focus is on the identification of competency gaps and an Individual Development Plan to address the gaps. They are supported with handholding by trainers and experts to work on relevant projects to implement learning and review progress with Sr. Management Members.

7. On the Talent Radar

The identification of high-potential talent is essential to ensure the growth and retention of existing employees in any organization. Hi-Potentials who exemplify the values and culture work closely with the Top Management/Sr. Management and are exposed to the values & culture of the organization at the source.

Through this approach, people are able to learn and experience the culture first hand and see how the Sr. Management operates. The secure communication that takes place between executives and employees ensures that there is no fear of communicating with seniors.

8. Employee Compensation

A right employee benefits package is affordable for both you and the company and comes with several options, all of which are met to help an employee stay focused on their job, and not how to protect themselves and their family.

High paid salaries are the first consideration that makes employees to seek shift. It's common to believe for all of us that we've been appropriately and fairly paid for the work we perform within an organization. You need to be sure to research what other businesses and organizations are providing concerning benefits and salaries.

It may be evident to some employers, but for every manager that is certain that competitive salary promotes employee engagement, several others have no clue.

Paying people a fair amount for the work they are doing, offering competitive compensation, benefits, and equitable working conditions will have a positive effect on employee morale.

Likewise, it's advisable to research the criteria compensation package and benefits for a particular position, especially retirement, health and accidental insurance, and paid benefits. You must ensure that the compensation package your organization has is highly competitive enough so that employees won't think of considering your rivals option.

9. Motivate people to leave their comfort zones

Very few of us will get thrilled about doing the same tasks daily. Provide a set of new tasks and responsibilities to grow and develop by leaving their comfort zones. The employee will also feel cherished, and even the employer may find to discover new talent and skills.

10. Discover Potential and Interests of the employees

Successful leaders discover people's talents and potentials working in the organization. Each individual has the capability and energy within them than they could ever think of. Your role, as a leader, would be to discover this truth for the benefit of your company as well as yourself.

When you are able to discover people's potential, you will be able to help them develop it so they can become more skillful and productive. There is absolutely no better service than helping other people to achieve excellence and become better individuals.

11. Help Them Move Up and Grow

Empowering leaders always think about how they can assist their fellow employees to grow. They consider ways they could guide men and women in developing new abilities. They delegate tasks, explain expectations, and coach them to triumph.

Empowering leaders always accept responsibilities for failure. Likewise, they do enable individuals to attempt new things without being concerned about failure, take larger steps without contending with other people, and climb the ladder up in their area without worrying about someone yanking them off the ladder.

By enabling other employees to do more than they think they can do at times, you have already guaranteed sure shot success.

12. Encourage Leadership

The ultimate role of an effective leader is to create more exemplary leaders. The right strategy for employee development is geared towards developing potential leaders who will affect many lives in positive ways.

Encouraging individuals to take up leadership roles, and lead by example should be of topmost priority in the list of employee development goals for any company that wants to attain the peak of success in this 21st century.

8.3 Health & Wellness

1. Unlimited Medical Leaves

Health is an invaluable commodity, and thus, some organizations, apart from their annual privilege leaves, organizations are started offering unlimited paid medical leave(s) to employees. By allowing unlimited paid medical leaves, the organization trusts its people and cares for them more than just a resource.

Employees aren't worried about sick days and will take the time they need to recover from the medical problems and then come back to work healthy and productive. By allowing unlimited paid medical leave, the organization trusts its people and cares for them more than just a resource.

2. Yoga Sessions

To have peace of mind & body of employees, every morning 15-30 minutes Yoga Session by a trained yoga teacher is beneficial for well being. Yoga provides an immediate return on investment through profound stress reduction, reduced anxiety, improved feelings of health & wellbeing, reducing absenteeism, and improved productivity. Depending upon the size of the organization, clusters can be made for yoga sessions and can be done in the open areas, preferably in the garden if available.

3. The rising importance of Health & Wellness

Employee Wellness made increasingly far-reaching Corporates have started to acknowledge how much employee wellness contributes towards the development of the organization. At the point when employees are focused on free and upbeat, they are significantly more beneficial.

Organizations should set up innovative methodologies to guarantee that the prosperity of their workforce is comprehensive. The meaning of wellness needs to extend to incorporate physical well-being, yet additionally mental, monetary, and otherworldly wellness.

It's very important for HR to conduct Free Health Check-up for all employees once or twice in a year depending on the size of the organization as well as should call in Doctors/Psychiatrists for seminars on various topics chosen by employees via a poll or depending on the medical problems at that time. Regular Blood donation camps in the organization can also be arranged as a part of social services.

4. Hospitals Tie-up for discounted Medical facilities

To provide better Health Care Services for the employees and their family members, employers have started tying up with the various big Hospitals on a country level(depending on the work locations/offices of the organization) to have better services & discounts on Doctor OPD/Consultation Fees, Investigations, Room Charges, Ambulance services etc. If any of employee or his family members want to avail, the health care discounted services from the tied up/network hospitals/their branches, and they can avail the same from the respective hospital by showing Employee Company ID Card. In the case of dependents/ family members, the employee shall have to show the ID Proof of concerned family members for establishing his/ her relationship with the employee.

It will also help employees for hassle-free medical treatment as well as saving some money too for self or in case of illness of any of the family members.

5. Gym

A free gym membership plan or membership discount vouchers are common things to offer to employees by the organization nowadays. Some companies even have a free gym facility on their properties, making it incredibly convenient for employees to use the facilities of the gym for their health and well-being. Generally, some of these gyms in the organizations have more than just a treadmill, weight lifting and exercise machines.

Employees can use the facilities of the gym before or after office hours or even in lunch or tea breaks. So employees have no excuse to exercise now!

6. Reduced work hours for new mothers

Reduce Half day/Half work weeks for New Mothers for initial 2-3 months to special take of her child also to get proper rest. Reduced working hours will also help new mothers to have more time to bond with their newly born babies and is also beneficial for breastfeeding.

This practice will be given immense feelings to the mother towards the organization, and the motivation and engagement towards the organization would be at an exceptional level.

7. Safety at the workplace

Safety is significant in employee engagement working in any organization. Employees should feel that their health should not be at risk as a result of their position in their respective work areas. Necessary tools like a mask, safety shoes, gloves, earbuds, helmet, etc. should be provided to employees working in areas that are risky to health such as Paint shop, fabrication line, etc.

This also helps the organization to have zero or negligible chances of industrial accidents, especially in manufacturing plants, construction sites, etc. When an organization feels about the safety of their employees, employees in return also feel good towards the organization.

8. Meditation Breaks

Meditation is being practiced from hundreds of the year, and proven technique for mental health. Meditation is one of the most common stress & anxiety reduction techniques used by people. Stress management should be a significant part of any workplace health & wellness program.

Taking 10-15 minutes break for meditation during the day can help employees de-stress and refocus their energies for improved productivity. Moreover, it will not involve any monetary expenses to the organization.

9. Mid-day fitness

Encourage employees to take small – small breaks on regular intervals to keep them refreshed. This is essential for employees having a higher degree of sitting in their jobs, especially working in Finance & Accounts, IT, Customer Support, Call Centers, Software programmers, banking professionals, etc. The most significant portion of any Health and Wellness Program is the Physical Activity. The small breaks help in

- The ability to think clearer
- Better decision-making skills
- It allows more brain space for genuine creative inspiration
- Taking breaks helps give your mind time to store information, so your memory recall is better
- Relaxation to the Eyes (especially working on computers)

Some companies have started offering on-site fitness classes during breaks or lunch hours.

10. Bicycle Friendly workplace

Promoting a bicycle-friendly workplace can bring a lot of encouraging health benefits. The truth is that through daily cycling will result into

- improve your cardiovascular health
- boost fitness
- increased muscle strength & flexibility
- decreased stress levels
- improved posture and coordination
- decreased body fat levels

Bicycle rides give a wide range of advantages to an individual's wellbeing, just as for the external environment in the form of reduced pollution. In addition, one can easily save some money too.

11. Sick Meals

Sick leaves will keep getting longer if employees don't recover soon. Speedy recovery is well supported by proper rest and healthy food. While all employers do provide sick leave to their employees so that they can recover and heal soon and even some of the companies providing unlimited medical leaves too.

Once employee re-joins the organization after medical leave, provide sick meals to them so as to regain their original strength more quickly as an employee spends on an average 8-9 hours in the organization. It enhances employees' morale and bonding with the organization.

12. Recognize the impact of stress

Help people to understand the difference between pressure and stress. A certain amount of pressure is essential for motivation, whereas too much or too little pressure leads to stress. It is important that everyone recognizes their own pressure limits and learns how to maintain a healthy amount of pressure in their day.

For someone to be as an engagement leader, it is very important to be aware that for many employees, the economic background will be adding external pressure, increasing worry, and reducing their capacity to work. To minimize the impact on your organization, encourage people to identify and recognize their current stressors, and build self-awareness.

13. Nap Times

After having a productive morning in the organization, after having lunch in the afternoon, almost every employee on the world is in an everlasting condition of sleepiness and is not actually productive as used to be in the morning hours or hours before lunch. Almost every employee can feel this in the organization.

However, the Japanese have a solution/ answer to this sleepiness problem!

In Japan, the maximum numbers of organizations are offering their employees nap time, convinced that it leads to better work performance after lunch hours and outcomes are successful, so far.

Okuta, a home renovation firm near Tokyo (Japan), allows its employees in the organization to take a 20-minute power nap at their work desks or in the staff lounge. This is introduced a few years back on the orders of the firm's chairman, Isamu Okuta, and it has proved an enormous hit.

8.4 Alignment

"The best companies now know, without a doubt, where productivity — real and limitless productivity — comes from. It comes from challenged, empowered, excited, rewarded teams of people. It comes from engaging every single mind in the organization, making everyone part of the action, and allowing everyone to have a voice — a role — in the success of the enterprise. Doing so raises productivity, not incrementally, but by multiples."

— Jack Welch

1. Management Feedback Day

Schedule an evening or 2 hour session in a month with the management in which the employees can ask the top management representatives about the issues that they are facing, know about the company's strategy, planning to basically ask the management anything that they want to know about the company or convey their grievances also (if any). This will result in improved alignment of an employee with the organization.

2. Monthly town hall meeting

Have a monthly town hall meeting in the organization, the objectives of which to have:

- Set & Convey goals and expectations
- Provide regular feedback
- Permit
- Employees control and occupation self-governance where possible
- Create an atmosphere of ownership
- Open announcement
- Steadily communicate the great things accomplished by the company and specific employees or teams
- Share how employees make a difference
- Share organizational, managerial challenges and problems and ask for their ideas. Make sure the employee recognizes how their performance influences the organization.

In short, create an atmosphere of mutually shared respect and appreciation and showed genuine interest in the employee as an individual.

3. E-Magazine

The E-Magazine (Digital Magazines) will help the employees in unlocking the gates of their creativity. Rightly said, human beings are blessed with creativity, which has added meaning and enjoyment to human life. The magazine will act as a platform to learn, share knowledge among the employees. The magazine might serve as an attempt to improve the working environment of the company by increasing the involvement of the employees.

Key benefits of E-Magazine

- A platform to share the monthly achievements/ accomplishment in the large organizations having multiple units and branches.

- Easier to circulate

- Company Branding (Both Internal and External branding)

- Will help in improving the working environment

- Encourage employees to unleash their potential

- Encourage employee's creative and innovative power for continuous improvement.

4. Resources

Provide employees with systems, tools, software that can make the job easier to do or which are the essential requirements of the job. Without the right mix of weapons, how one can expect to win the war...?

Just for example, for the people working in the "Store department" of any organization, it will be far more convenient and time-saving to maintain the inventory of items in inventory software than to manage physical register or maintain in the word file or excel. This inventory software will save the huge time of employees in keeping the inventories and also without any discrepancies.

This way, you'll get them to invest their energy into doing great work, instead of wasting precious time.

5. Case Studies

Give the employee real-life case studies. This will help the employees in improving decision-making abilities in different real-life cases. They will also understand the value of decisions taken by management, which many times employees think not favorable to them.

The same can be done with teams also i.e., providing real-life case studies to the team and ask them to submit their action plan of that case. This will also improve the decision-making abilities of the employees in different cases.

6. Connect Them On Social Media

These days, most of the employees are using social media to connect with coworkers. Help your candidates (prospect employees) to connect to the company and colleagues on social media as soon as they've been officially hired or given offer letters (Letter of Intent). It will help in getting them involved with company culture & values before they even set foot in the organization's door (and it's also an excellent way to help build a social presence for your brand).

Moreover, this will certainly improve the chances of joining of a candidate in the organization and not backing out after taking out an offer letter.

7. Share stories

Sharing stories about how employees' work impacts customers and the organization will help the employees to rethink their doing/actions at the workplace, keeping customers and organization in mind.

8. Role Clarity

As part of a smooth induction process, provide Role/ Goal Sheet to all new employees at the time of their joining in the Organization. A well-defined Roles & Responsibilities helps the employee in understanding exactly what is expected from him/her and what are their key accountabilities in the organization and will enable them to perform better in their assigned roles.

9. Make Buzz

Launching a new project/product is a very exciting time for any company irrespective of its size and nature and even a portion of the product – will begin to create a buzz of excitement in the organization.

And a company only thrives when employees are motivated to make it as a success — so creating excitement about upcoming projects/products of the company by emails, notice boards, etc. The employee feels delighted and aligned with the organization in waiting for the upcoming projects/products.

10. Employees Survey

Every four to six months, conduct an employee survey where all our employees provide input on the health of the workplace in the organization. This survey enables the organization to identify how strongly the employees feel about the organization and how strong is the employee clarity of his/her existence deliverables in the organization. Employees survey also helps in employees own ability to co-relate with organizational Mission, Vission, and future plans.

In an employee survey, one can also reveal whether he feels that his supervisor takes an interest in his personal & professional development, or has received any word of praise from the immediate boss for a good job done (if any) and so on. This proves to be an eye-opener for the managers as well.

11. Clearly Defined Management Roles

Employees at any level should know about the hierarchy of the organization possessing who they report to, and managers & Departmental heads should know who reports to them. To some, this sounds observable. You can't be a great manager if you don't know who you manage, and having clear management roles is one-way companies can enable great leadership

12. Putting the Right Talent for the Right Job

Putting the right talent in the right position can radically increase employees' retention and enriches the company's success by decreasing costs in several business aspects.

You need to discover the way by which you can make your employee performs better by placing them in a domain where they can be truly helpful.

A brand new car behind glass is only a mass of metal glass and plastic, but a car being pushed is truly what a car ought to be. The same goes for employees. Once developed, one ought to use what they have learned so that they can turn the world around them a better place for others and themselves. Armed with this practice, do not neglect the area of coaching and training.

13. One to one meeting

Depending on the size & volume of the organization, Meet one-on-one with employees to talk about what they like and dislike about their job. Where organizations are large in size, the responsibility of one-on-one meetings can be passed down to Head of Department, Managers, and Line Leaders.

14. Well Defined Induction & orientation

Employee engagement begins right from joining of the employee in the organization; the first impact in the judgment of the employee is induction & orientation. This is the foremost responsibility of the HR Department to have influenced the joining of the new incumbents. The HR Department strives ahead in enabling the new employees to become familiar with the work environment and all the terms & conditions, policies, and procedures that are followed at the workplace. Also, to give a brief idea of the benefits offered to the employees.

- The induction given should be simple to interpret but completed to create satisfaction in the minds of young employees. Necessary arrangements like arranging the induction room, snacks, induction material, etc. will be made.

- Employee Induction shall be equipped with all the following concerns:-

  - Organizational Mission, Vision & Culture

  - Information about the Product & Services

  - Briefing of the employees concerned department and Organization Structure

  - Company Payroll and Benefits

- Company Policies and Procedures

- One to one meeting with key employees in the organization

15. Create a positive working atmosphere

While benefits and compensations are relatively important, the primary motives employees leave an organization is also likened to the following factors such as unorganized work environment, toxic workplaces, bad bosses, and difficult co-workers, etc.

Every employee wants a clean, organized work environment in which they have the necessary equipment to perform well.

When resources and People aren't organized; physical barriers are put in the way of having the ability to work efficiently, obviously inducing anxiety. Endeavor to arrange things so that employees can have easy access to the people and resources they want.

This generally works best by organizing workspaces around workers operating the process, or the kinds of work that they do. The concept is to make it as simple as possible for employees to do their tasks.

Make certain that you describe to your employees why you are doing this. Highlight the advantages of making the change. The quality of mentorship and supervision, by a "bad boss" was said so often that, workers leave workers, not their own jobs.

Supervisors & Managers play the biggest role in staff development and organization successes. Employees are more likely to stay with an organization when they have a good and positive work atmosphere.

16. Job titles

When you consider a job title for an employee, be creative. Ask your employees to give you their input for the correct tile for a job. The right title is significant and enables a person to be proud of their position at the firm and work he/she is doing.

17. Try and try again

It's very important that you try (engagement leaders) and adapt until finding the perfect angle for your employee engagement strategy in the organization. There is 'N' number of activities and practices which can be deployed based on the need of the organization (some of the factors are explained in this book).

In fact, you can pick some activities from the book and apply it as per your organizational needs.

Keep on trying until you find perfect matches of your employee engagement strategy and success will be all yours.

18. Walk your talk

What leadership example do you set? Actions really do speak louder than words. You must lead yourself as you would have your team members lead. Let your employees see you living the principles of what your organization stands for. Follow through on your promises to gain your employees' trust.

A work culture that fosters trust and integrity will naturally create a committed and engaged workforce that stands firm in tougher times.

19. Have a commercial conversation with your employees

During economically challenging times, you need people to be making good profitable decisions every day. You need them to be aware of the costs of providing each service to customers, the revenues or budgets involved, and be selective about where they put their time and attention to give the best operational return.

Involving people closely in increasing revenues and decreasing costs can increase engagement and maximize competitive or operational advantage.

20. Allow Employees Focus

Employees need to realize that the work they're doing is being valued and foremost, what's more when given a chance that they do, they will be engaged with the organization.

So allow your employees to focus on what best they can do in the organization. If the opportunity is given to them to shine, they have the ability to do by doing their best as much as they are able to do.

The biggest mistake arises when the manager/supervisor assigns tasks to those who work under them that don't match their skill set, not only leads to poor performance but there will be no doubt having a negative influence on employee engagement.

If you want your employees to stay as engaged as possible, you have to allow them to focus on their skills.

21. Conduct Periodic Interviews

It is essential for employers to conduct interviews occasionally with their long-term employees to assess those employees' feelings about the way the company is managing them and what could be done to enhance these efforts, aside from the obvious exit and entrance interviews.

Conducting these Kinds of interviews equips the company with credible information about her needs and that of its employees and enables them to boost their efforts for better outcomes in the long run.

22. Discover their Potential and Interests

Successful leaders discover people's talents and potentials. Each individual has the capability and energy within them than they could ever think of. Your role, as a leader, would be to discover this truth for the benefit of your company as well as yourself.

When you are able to discover people's potential, you will be able to help them develop it so they can become more skillful and productive. There is absolutely no better service than helping other people to achieve excellence and become better individuals.

8.5 Collaboration

1. Feedback Culture

The power of Feedback is quite impressive. Building an excellent feedback culture at work can not only bring terrific innovation and productivity but also improves employee's motivation and engagement.

However, it's easier said than done. Human emotions, egos, hierarchies, and politics fester distrust among employees and prevent them from opening their minds. Setting up the right examples from top leadership can play a pivotal role in building a dominant feedback culture.

2. Festival Celebration

The Festival celebrations are the days to forgive and never look back, and to attempt to end clashes that may have arisen while working to achieve organizational goals. Could there be a superior day to make harmony among groups and individuals who are at loggerheads in the workplace? Over the course of time, this will translate into better collaboration and teamwork. There is a huge list of festivals around the world. According to the location and region of the workplace, festivals can be celebrated.

3. Employee Birthday celebration

The birthday celebration inculcates the feeling of belongingness and creates an employee-friendly/engaging environment in the organization by extending greetings to its all employees on the special occasions of their Birthdays. Depending upon the size & structure of the organization or work area (Brach Office, Marketing, Office, Head Quarters, Corporate Office, Regional Offices), a birthday celebration can be planned.

For smaller organizations or work areas (Office, Plant), the birthday of an employee can be celebrated on the same day. For large organizations/work area, Employee's birthday falling in a particular month can be celebrated jointly in the month-end (last week of the month), and Cake cutting ceremony should be arranged in the presence of Team Members and Heads of the organization. At this celebration, a Memento (Personalized Birthday Gift) or gift voucher can also be given to the respective employee as per the budget of the organization.

Discourage to discuss employees' problems on their official matters during the celebration, and employees will be encouraged to share their personal life / about family and how they feel in the organization. Moreover, they can share experiences about working in the organization.

I came across the company in which Sr. Employees Birthday is celebrated with family members. One HR person visits the home along with Cake and Bouquet and Cake cutting ceremony was done in the presence of a concerned employee, and his/her family members.

Let's have few lines of feedback collected from one of such Sr. Team Member-

"My Company never forgets to send Birthday Cake and bouquet to home on my Birthday. It's been an amazing feeling and makes me happy to be a part of such a caring employee organization"

—One of Satisfied Employee.

Birthday falling in a particular month, the name of employees with wishes can be displayed at companies notice board and can also be sent on a group email. Some of the organization, introduce the new joiners, followed by cake cutting ceremony and giving the gifts to the birthday buddies, this can be followed by few simple/jolly games and end the evening by giving some attractive prizes to those who win in the games and with some crucial announcements followed by snacks. It hardly takes a span of 2 hours.

Some of the activities which may be planned at the time of group birthday celebrations (once in a month):

- Dance/Song competition – Dance/song competition between birthday buddies.

- Movies Dumb Charades - Let any member pick a paper from the box or bowl that they have. One person from each team should come forward and read the content in the paper. He/she should make their other team members understand which movie name is there in the paper via actions alone (no verbal communication at all) if team members get what their team member was trying to tell then that team wins a small gift.

- Hit the pot - Tie a pot with colorful paper, and every member of a team should hit the pot within three strokes.

- Poetry corner - Best poetry presented by a member will be awarded.

- Catwalk – Birthday buddies do the catwalk, and the best one is awarded

- Sing-Along (Anthakshari) - Singing songs starting with the last letter of the song

- Hunt - Hide a small gift somewhere in the celebration hall. The gift belongs to the one who finds it.

- My story - Let audiences/ birthday buddies describe their daily activities right since they wake up till they sleep with actions alone. The best one will get a prize.

4. Make employees feel like they belong

Developing a proper strategy for employee growth and development is not achievable without full knowledge of your employees' desires, and potential. A perfect way to discover this is to adopt effective listening.

Through effective listening, it is possible to learn about people's fears, dreams, strengths, limiting beliefs, and ideas. In this manner, they will be able to get to the right track and assist them in what they want to do.

5. Transparency

Integrity and Transparency are crucial components of workplace ethics. Being honest and doing the right thing under all circumstances, ensuring that employees have easy access to information and encouraging open discussions strengthen the pillar of Trust. Organizations must firmly believe that employees have confidence that they can freely report concerns which will be investigated by Concerned Departmental Heads, with appropriate remedial action, and without fear or favor.

Escalation Matrices should be well defined so that timely appropriate action can be taken without a biased approach. To facilitate this approach, communicate to all employees from time to time to report any serious misconduct.

6. Departmental Get-Together

Departmental Get-together improves team building & cohesiveness among the employees. It will help in smooth coordination and increased bonding among different departments as well. This will help in doing their inter department's day to day jobs much more accessible.

Departmental get together can be organized once in a quarter/year depending upon the size of the organization, preferably outside the work area followed by lunch/dinner.

7. Grievance Handling System

Constitute a substantial Grievance Handling System to help the employee to resolve their grievances in the shortest span of time with satisfaction considering all facts and figures of the grievance. To resolve the grievances of employees at work and to provide a clear understanding of the grievance redressal procedure of the company. Any employee having any grievance pertaining to the work or behavior of his/her colleague/superior can contact his department manager for its redressal. The sample grievance mechanism is mentioned herewith (which can be taken as a reference to make the Grievance Handling mechanism in their organization as its process depends on the 'N' number of factors).

- It is the responsibility of his/her Departmental Manager to listen to his/her complaint/ grievance and redress the same within two days' time positively.

- If the Department Manager is not able to redress the grievance, then the complainant can approach the concerned HOD, and the HOD will redress the same within four days from its receipt.

- If the complainant is not satisfied with the decision of the HOD, he may approach the Business Head/Plant Head and who will redress the same within four days from its receipt.

- The Business Head/Plant Head will make all possible efforts to redress the grievance of the complainant, and if he so desires, he may discuss the complaint with the Corporate Head or chairman/director depending upon the hierarchy of the organization.

When the grievances of the employees are resolved to the utmost satisfaction, it results in improved collaboration of employees in the organization.

8. No Email Please

Have a no-email day once in a month for the employees of the same location, but different domains/departments will inspire employees to have in-person interaction.

This will help in the bonding of employees of different departments and may get to know each other personally, which will certainly help in doing their inter-departmental tasks much more easily. This activity will have improved Collobaration among the departments.

9. Thanksgiving Friday

It's time to appreciate your team member, team leader, team manager for any small support and rendering valuable help of time. Every Friday, give a small card or handwritten note for thanking them. It will be an encouraging and motivating factor for the receiving person.

10. Encourage Two-way communication

Encourage two-way communication by having a meeting with MD & HR quarterly or half-yearly depending upon the size of the organization. The MD and the HR head go to all the branch offices and work locations of the organization to let their people know about the business and request the people's involvement in fulfilling the organization's goals mutually. HR head discusses & communicates talks about the new HR policies & practices, and then there is an open discussion for issues related to HR or other organizational issues.

Employees can express themselves on whatever issues (directly or indirectly relating to them) they have with regard to work in the organization. If there are sensitive issues in the organization, which they don't want to discuss openly, they can write and give those without their names. Make sure to work on the genuine issues raised by the employees; otherwise, this will not be on any use.

11. Networking

Invite top performers of the organization to attend a networking or special event with senior leaders. This will help in improving interpersonal skills enhanced communication skills of the employees resulting in a higher degree of collaboration among the employees. Also, an extraordinary employee is one who is driven and centered around improving his or her own talent; however much as could be expected.

Urging your employees to network with others (both inside and outside of your association) is an extraordinary method to enable them to concentrate on structure their professions, at the same time helping them to be increasingly occupied with their present jobs.

The potentials are never-ending, and the more your employees focus on structuring their networks in some or other way, the more your business will benefit in the end.

12. Sports club

A different team for playing team-building sports like Cricket, Basketball, Football, Volley Ball, etc. teams are formed between employees and matches are conducted & winning team is awarded. Taking back the fun concept of 'House Teams,' each employee is randomly assigned one of the five households and is allotted a budget for activities and initiatives for the year. Apart from House Teams, a team based on different Business Divisions of the organization can also be made depending upon the size of the organization.

Various competitions are hosted between the houses and the one with the maximum points is awarded the 'Best House' trophy. This cross-functional communication amongst employees fosters companionship and teamwork within the organization.

This will be very cost-friendly, and the employees will also get a chance to improve their relations beyond the office and also remain fit and healthy.

13. Allow Employees Work in other Departments

By allowing your employees to move around from one department to another on occasionally, this will not only enable employees to get to know employees of other departments better, but everyone will begin to see the different system & processes in which the business indeed runs for which they are not aware of.

This naturally leads to a more engaged workforce, and each employee who is allowed to work in other departments will bring with him the information they take away from working in other different departments to apply it to their own position. It's truly a win-win situation, and more than worth experimenting with.

14. Fear free workplace environment

So many businesses and companies tend to operate at a performance-driven environment free from any fear.

This sort of environment atmosphere is a favorable environment.

Allowing your employees to make choices without any sort of fear and having to run everything, allows them great moments within their career. Coincidentally, these performance-based environments can also lead to the fear of getting scolded if their decision falls flat. Managing a business where employees are punished for mistakes or a wrong choice is a sure-fire strategy for staff to become disengaged and unwilling to take risks sometimes necessary for success.

15. Team Meeting

Department wise team will be conducted by HR where in which each employee comes up with new thoughts and ideas to improve the Quality of work, also how to deliver the product & services on time, how to reach out for customer satisfaction, technology growth, the significance of teamwork, knowledge on advanced technologies, etc. At the end of the meet, the department head nominates an employee and gifts him a prize for his innovative and creativeness. This helps the employees to come with good ideas, thereby showing their creative skills.

16. A Matter of Trust

Earning trust between employees, supervisors, and senior management will only help boost employee engagement. The higher a person is in the organization; the more their decisions will be examined, to see how their accomplishments affect the overall direction of the organization.

For developing outstanding leaders-and promoting engagement in workers-they must be firm and principled; then the trust will develop.

17. Involve employees in the improvement program

Nothing is more disappointing to an employee than realizing how to take care of an issue; however, being un-engaged to do as such. Start involving employees in the improvement programs planned in the organization. Employees who realize that their ideas & thoughts are taken care of seriously by the management results in a sign of encouragement to them.

Moreover, the employees who were directly working on the issues might have a better improvement plan in place.

8.6 Motivation & Encouragement

1. Marriage Gift (Shagun)

Marriage Shagun (Wedding Gift) is given to employees at the time of marriage of self as well as the marriage of family members (Daughter, Son, Sister, Brother). Marriage Shagun can be given in the form of cash amount, vouchers, gift items, companies, personalized gifts. The same can be given in the marriage ceremony by Departmental Head, his/her colleagues or HR person. The employees will feel proud to be associated with the organization who gives a nice gesture on the auspicious occasion of their self or marriage in a family.

2. Employer Branding

A satisfies and engaged employee creates a positive image of the organization in both internal & external worlds. Employee engagement leads to value-added internal branding of the organization that in turn aids in:-

- Increased Employee Retention
- Highly ranked for Employer attractiveness
- Increased level of staff engagement
- Lower recruitment costs
- Minimized loss of talented employees
- Employees recommending the organization as a "preferred" place to work
- Employees committed to organizational goals
- Shorter recruitment time

3. Time-bound HR Services

Especially in the large organizations having a multifold presence, its necessary to ensure timely services to all the Employees of the company on various HR related issues, well defined separate responsibilities have been given to each HR Team member. Responsibility metrics of each HR team member and their contact details (Email ID, Mobile Number & Landline Number) to enable the Employees to access/reach to the concerned HR Person pertaining to the corresponding/concern HR responsibility area is being sent to all employees of the company on their email id's on regular intervals.

Escalation Matrix is also being shared with all employees of the company so that issues (if any) can be sorted in a time-bound manner.

It helps the employee to sort out their issues related to HR in a hassle-free manner, thus improving the motivation of the employees.

4. Travel Incentives

Motivating employees, especially highly competitive employees working on the production lines, office works can be a challenging task. Sure, everyone likes money, but what if you could offer an incentive that worth more than money? That's what travel incentives are all about. Can you imagine what would generate more excitement among your employees; offering Rs. 20K or 2nights stay in Goa including Airfare? I'll bet that you didn't have to think about which one to choose.

5. Equal Opportunity Policy

If any employee is recruited with some disability, the Company should strive to maintain a work environment that is friendly to the person with a disability, including but not limited to – making of ramps, disability-friendly toilets, seating plan and other suitable arrangements which might be required for smooth working by such employees. These small-small kinds of stuff will make employees working a lot easier and feel encouraged and happy to be part of the organization who takes care of their employees.

6. Well defined HR Policies

Well established and equally implemented set of HR policies are crucial for any organization. Employees behave encouraged when they are treated with the same set of policies and procedures without any biased approach. Whenever there is any update to an ongoing HR policy, or a new policy is incorporated, it must be appropriately communicated to his employees in the organization through email, notice board, print or e-magazines, etc.

7. Celebrate achievements

Celebrate achievements, whether it is financial or non-financial. Employees need to feel encouraged and that they are regarded as part of the organization. The leadership team needs to indicate the amount they care for their employees and show acknowledgment for endeavors.

Its rightly said - "Employees don't leave a company; they leave their manager." If you want to reduce employee turnover in the organization, improve the competency and quality of managers. The lack of employee engagement is a real problem, but effective managers can make a difference.

8. Charity

Give employees a paid day off once in a while to volunteer at a charity or non-profit organization of their choice. This will help in encouraging charity among the employees as well as activities that will boost the self-esteem of the employees.

9. E-greetings

E-greetings have been operational many organizations through the intranet to send appreciation to other employees. Special cards suited to the occasion are made available. This is a good way of recognizing and appreciating employees in the organization, especially the employee who find face to face recognition somehow uncomfortable.

10. Workplace flexibility

Organization policies need to be a little flexible either by giving your employees the choice to work flexible hours or do some personalize schedule rotations or a self-scheduling through coordinating with some other staff in-charge are sure ways of promoting and boosting employee morale. You could also allow your employees to leave work early to attend to a personal matter as appropriate.

Workplace flexibility is sometimes difficult to manage since you need to meet some operational requirements.

To manage workplace flexibility, a policy should be well defined and be implemented accordingly, so its' good intent will not be lost in meeting operational demands.

11. Allow employees to personalize their workspace

It will help employees to personalize their workplace, according to their preference, which might work with them as a boosting factor. This activity will not incur any cost or just negligible cost to the employer as well. So allow employees to personalize their workplace as long as it's done in the right spirit and does not carry any negative impact on other employees of work areas.

12. Employee Confirmation

Practice Confirming employees (No Probation period) from the first day of joining. The absence of a probation period in the appointment letter will improve the trust of the employee as well as responsibility towards the organization.

13. Hire A Business Motivational Speaker

The opportunity arrives when they have to lift your employees' motivation emerges. When giving incentives and perks not to work any longer, Top leadership team/ engagement, leaders resort to contracting a business motivational speaker. Welcoming such a speaker to a company occasion is an ideal opportunity to offer your employees a reprieve from the everyday task.

It might require extra funds for your company as hiring a motivational speaker could be expensive. However, the countless helpful tools that a speaker can provide your employees with would be worth all the money. More so, when your employees learn that a top caliber and in the black keynote speaker comes over your company gathering to inspire them, they will recognize the extra attention and expense you are willing to spend on their behalf.

14. Cute baby contest

The cute baby contest is an employee's kids' competition. The employee's kids also got a chance to see the organization where their parents also work an opportunity to perceive the products and services.

Not to forget to give something to every kid apart from winners in the form of consolation prizes/gifts.

15. Inspire People

There might be no better way to motivate and inspire employees by the bottom of the heart than bringing out and highlighting internal stories of success! The employees who have demonstrated exceptional performance and growth in the organization can be an integral part of the internal stories.

Each month these members are interviewed by the HR team, and these stories are documented and shared across all locations. In addition, the interviews are also displayed on the notice boards at each plant. The series serves as an excellent recognition tool and an inspiration to the young fast trackers in the organization.

16. New recruits workstation

Decorate workstation of new recruits with balloons and ribbons. New family members of the organization feel excited and privileged to be part of an employee-centric organization. The feeling about the organization he/she will take while returning home would be amazing.

17. Crèche Facility

A crèche or a daycare facility should be started with a small room, and a babysitter wherein the women of the company would take lesser leaves. They will be satisfied as their baby would be well taken care of in or near to working areas. The facility assures the employees that their kids are in the right hands while they are at work.

18. Exam Support Leave

Organizations might often forget to give importance to the personal life of their employees, but some organizations are setting a great example in that space. All employees of the organization whose children are appearing for 10th/12th standard board examinations are entitled to avail a 7-days of examination support leave. It is a beautiful step to show the employees as well as their families about how much organization really cares for them. Afterward, the organization realizes that parents are as anxious for their children's board exams and deserve a happy chance to endure them!

19. Regard and respect each employee as an individual

You need to recognize your employees' contributions in front of other members of the organization. This can lessen the tendency for employees to believe that their supervisors take all of the praise and credits.

Learn how to recognize your employees, not all employees like to be singled out at a gathering of hundreds of contemporaries.

A simple pat at the back given frequently can significantly boost employee morale. Most times, employees will appreciate the time you invested in locating them in their desk, and they will deliver the message.

20. Retirement Plans

Employees who are in the phase of retirement in the coming years to come or employees are nearing retirement; consider allowing them to invest their funds in the retirement plans. They can be given programs, investing their funds wisely so as to get most of it without worrying about the financial aspect in the future.

21. Paternity Leaves

Luckily, more men today need to be associated with their Child's first weeks at home, and companies are beginning to express their help for paternity leave. A few organizations are starting to see the adjustment in culture, offering in any event, unpaid paternity leaves notwithstanding maternity leave.

Maybe it's not necessarily on compliance part, but companies are showing how much it is important now as part of their employee engagement initiatives.

22. Dinner with Music

For enhancing the motivation & performance of the employees

You may have yearly dinner with music where all employees from top to bottom attend the event, and the communication barriers between hierarchy also reduced.

It creates a positive culture because employees feel that management cares about them.

23. Employee Empowerment

Employees want to know that they can be trusted to make decisions. That they have a voice in the decision making and goal setting. Often when given the opportunity, they will stretch their goals. Employee empowerment provides an employee with a feeling of encouragement and motivation.

Empowered employees possess a sense of responsibility and a feeling of ownership, and their ideas are usually recognized.

So workplaces that promote empowerment over what and how things are being done and the perception that they are relevant to the organization will yield outstanding productivity results and few complaints.

Once employees have the notion that they also need their organization as much as the organization needs them, then they would be best valued more than a paycheck and also all benefits package that convinces them to stay and remained in the organization for a longer period.

24. Stay Interviews

The most aspect of any successful HR practices and employee engagement is employee retention. It basically represents the ability of the company to retain its performing employees. Companies nowadays are focusing on Exit Interviews, which helps in accessing the key concerns and motivating factors that encouraged them to leave the current organization. This not only helps in knowing the positive factors which drive employees to stay with the organization but also, gives an idea about steps that can make them more productive and engaged with the organization.

25. Plan Properly

Organizations without plans suffer greatly. Unfortunately, many organizations don't put a proper plan in place for the growth of their employees and organization.

Personal development deficient of proper planning normally leads to conflicts both internally and externally. This, in turn, leads to less motivation, decline productivity, and a huge loss in a variety of ways.

When the Ideal plan for development is created based on the workers' desires, needs, and potential, the expected positive result will definitely be achieved.

26. Balance Work and Personal Life

Human resource professionals are rising up to the challenges of a transforming company workforce reality that the need to know about certain tendencies that influence efforts to attract and keep talented employees.

Applying work-life balance to one's effective private life and work-life was not as critical before as it is today. Why? Because, in the past, people are able to attend to every major task in their lifetime.

Family is essential to all employees; when work starts to put a huge strain on one's household, no huge amount of money will be able to keep an employee around.

Therefore tiny gestures of permitting an employee to take a protracted leave once a month to watch with his son's or daughter's school activity will likely be replaced with protracted employment and loyalty within an organization.

8.7 Happiness

"Clients do not come first. Employees come first. If you take care of your employees, they will take care of the clients."

—Richard Branson

1. Involvement in CSR activities

The involvement of employees in CSR activities, published in a local newspaper would be encouraging and result in improved social belongingness. Make employees part of the CSR group. This also shows them that you are constructing an organization that cares about the social community, which can have an encouraging effect on the employees.

2. Casual dress

Have casual dress Fridays (Organizations with five-day working) and casual dress Saturdays (Organizations with six days working). Get them out from their formal dress suit & tie to T-Shirt & Jeans or whatever they feel comfortable in wearing. Casual Dress codes can have a massive impact on attitude; who wishes to be in a shirt and pants all day long? Even though the dress code in the workplace helps maintain a sense of professionalism, by allowing a casual attire day, allow your employees to experience more relaxed and comfortable throughout the daytime.

3. Cheer Personal projects

Allow employees a short time of up to 20-30 minutes in a day to work on their own projects like their personal diary, children's work, bank work, personal emails, etc.

It can trigger creativity and energy flow that would only benefit the rest of the working hours. At this time, they will quickly finish off the personal project; otherwise, they may think of doing it all times in a day.

4. Give them a Break

A full-time job is very tiring & exhausting, and by the end of a workday, your employees are probably exhausted too much. The best things once can do to keep them motivated and to reward them is to provide them with ways to take a small break from work for 30 minutes or so, such as with things like, snacks, games, reading the material, a gym or a TV. No matter how much your employees enjoy their job, a full 8+ hours workday can be challenging. Even more challenging in the organizations which have six days working week.

5. Snack bars

Mid-morning and mid-afternoon employees feel those pangs of hunger, where they need a beverage or a snack to keep them going. Most office buildings have a vending machine with the typical candy and soda cans available. Some companies even offer snack bars with much more variety and healthier options available, sometimes even for free.

6. Games

Some companies offer a game room, maybe combined with the TV room. Pool and video games, such as Wii, are some of the games available for employees to play. 15-20 minutes of quick break for games are great stress relievers for any age group.

7. Loan Schemes

Loans are given as an aid to monetary help to the employees for different needs without any financial inconvenience. The loan can be given to employees as per specific grades and salary levels and one a time. Request for a new loan application can only be considered if the previous loan was settled/paid off. Types of Loan-

- For purchasing Car
- For purchasing Bike
- Education Loan for pursuing higher studies or for the education of children (s).
- For renovation or purchasing of Home
- Laptop Loan
- Family Vacation
- Medical Issues
- Marriage of self or in the family

Loans help the employees to fulfill their needs without any financial difficulty. When this is taken care of by the organization, employees are more than happy in working.

8. Establish a Fun Committee

Every company has its own unique culture, values, and diversity, and fun activities that work in one organization might not work in another organization. Establishing a fun committee not only helps assure that fun activities and events will actually be created and implemented from time to time; it assures that they will be appropriate for your company also. The fun committee should rotate to keep ideas fresh and sustain an ongoing commitment to fun on the job.

9. Recognize a personal accomplishment

Recognize a personal accomplishment or milestone in the life of employees, such as the birth of children, weddings of self or in family, retirements, marriage anniversaries, and professional development achievements. When an organization recognizes the personal accomplishment, the employee feels connected with the organization.

10. Office Theme

Creating theme days at the workplace in the organization is an effective way to relax people up and create an enjoyable environment at their workplace. Have themed office days as this initiative can bring a great deal of fun and gain employee commitment to the organization. Theme office days can be crazy hair day, Fairytale Friday, Theatre Sunday, Sports Dress, etc.

Also theme-based quarterly or half-yearly or annually as per the organization size and culture, theme-based event serves as an exciting and participative program to bring out employees' talents and build a culture of learning, development, and teamwork. Each event should be based on a theme.

11. Support Employee in personal Situations

Employees should be supported especially the ones who are going through a tough phase of life at the moment.

It could be due to Medical issues with him or in family, family issues, financial loss, etc. This is the time when they need someone to back upon. Try to provide the best possible help one can give to the concerned employee in the organization.

12. Work Anniversaries

There is no better way to motivate employees than celebrating employee work anniversaries; give employees a gift and a card on their work anniversary. If budget is an issue, only a card will bring the same encouragement to the employees on their work anniversaries as any other gift can do. Depending upon the organization size, work anniversaries can be celebrated jointly in a month or as and when it arises.

13. Drum Jam Activity

It is a fun and exciting, corporate team outing activity. There is no need for segregating the team into smaller groups. Instead, music plays and drum beats are felt. The activity is aimed at reducing the stress that builds up gradually while working in a highly competitive work environment.

It boosts team morale and helps the team works in perfect tandem as a cohesive whole. The communication between the team improves.

14. Surprise special meal in the canteen on special occasions

Plan Surprise special meal in the canteen on special occasions like foundation day, special religious days, Birthday of Leadership Team, etc. The employees will get to know about the occasion as well as feel privileged to be part of a special gesture.

15. Loyalty Grows With Happiness

Employees in the organization are more likely to remain loyal and demonstrate cohesiveness in the long run with the organization if they are happy at the workplace. The organization should undertake a host of measures to ensure the happiness of the employee at all times. This will also help in improved morale and satisfaction of the employee.

8.8 Acceptance

1. Idea Generation in Sales

Introduce "Idea Generation for higher Sales" as competition in your organization. Ask every employee in the organization to contribute their innovative ideas to increase sales of various products and services the company. Collect all ideas and then select the best ones out of them and implement them. The idea for generating the highest sales wins the competition and award is given to the contributor of the award. This will also encourage other employees to contribute their ideas in such competitions, which will help the organization increase its profits.

2. Help in the hell is helping indeed

Offer to help those employees who aren't performing well. One can't expect every member of his/her team to perform at an exceptional level and be an outstanding achiever at all times. There are going to be few individuals that need a helping hand, especially if they're new to the organization or are puzzled on a particular project.

Giving special attention to employees who are not performing well will not only fix the problem, but it shows that you care enough to help who is in desperate need. Every manager is busy for a time and doesn't use this as an excuse to neglect to help the employees when they are running into the issues.

3. Keep Them In The Know

It's essential to keep the employees updated who are posted at different locations and branches regarding significant projects, goals, accomplishments, and a lot more for the company. Develop an employee-friendly goal setting, tracking, and feedback system to give everyone access to company goals, progress updates, new projects, and more. More than that, ask for their insight, advice, and preferences.

Nobody in an organization likes to be being kept in the dark; having specific goals and an expectation, providing tools and resources to perform the job is the backbone of employee engagement.

4. Suggestion box

Being part of the process, knowing their ideas matter and feeling they have input in the way their job is performed is a trademark of an engaged, involved employee. Do not forget; they are the ones in the trenches. Feedback and brainstorming-and are actually implementing bright ideas, no matter where they come from-will ensure employee participation.

Suggestion box at the cafeteria or any other commonplace can be kept and idea's should be invited. Only the suggestions for improvement of internal procedures (with or without a name) should be encouraged & gossips, personal comments are discouraged. New ideas are inspired by displaying their names & ideas in the company notice board. Suggestions can be given one or more in the following areas:

- Deviation in any policy or procedure or any contradiction therein.

- Reduction in waste

- Service & Quality improvement

- Process simplification

- Cost-saving

- Time-saving

- Energy Saving

- Improvement in productivity

- Improvement in product design

- Improvement in safety standards

- Work simplification in sales, marketing, account, etc.,

- Good Housekeeping

- Any other suggestion is leading to improvement.

5. Employees Late Sitting

Employees as much as possible; need to be discarded late sitting in the respective work area. If it's extremely necessary to work late, employers must provide extra facilities to the employees who might be sitting late hours at their workplaces for the company's important work. Some examples are given here as under and can act as a reference to make late sitting guidelines so as to take care of work and not to incubate the feeling of disengagement among the employees.

- Employees are sitting late up to 1 Hour beyond normal working hours, will be provided with tea.

- Employees sitting late from 1 hour to 3 hours, will be provided with snacks like Burger, Chips, Patties, Bread, Sandwiches, Biscuits, etc.

- Employees sitting late beyond 3 hours from their normal working hours, will be provided with dinner by the Company. Company conveyance can also be provided for employees sitting late at night and don't have their own transportation.

If we do something extra for employees while he is sitting late to meet the operational needs, it will not carry disengagement in the employee.

6. Employee participation

Ensure employee's involvement in developing the organization's mission, vision, values, and strategic direction. Employees feel privileged being part of a team in creating an organizational vision, mission, and values and also an acknowledgment to the employees is exceptionally guaranteed.

7. Highlight Employee

Highlight/Feature a different employee in each internal newsletter/Print Magazine or E-magazine. This will be a great booster for employees, mainly at Junior or middle levels. Small bio and accomplishment/key skills can be part of this employee booster section of the magazine.

8. You need to be engaged in your employees for them to be engaged in their job

If you treat employees as "just another employee," then they will treat you as "just another job." The best talent has to be nurtured and encouraged from the bottom of the heart. The point is that you need to be engaged in your employees for them to be engaged in their job. Organized processes, great management, and growth opportunities are among the most important things to employees today. To find out what matters to your employees, all you have to do is ask their feedback.

9. Foster Communication and Availability

The HR department needs to be somewhat receptive to employee concerns. In many organizations, the HR division is charged with the responsibilities of making organization policies.

In fact, the Human resources department, responsiveness to employee demands is one of the cornerstones.

You can easily do so by actively listening to your employees. Give them honest feedback, whether negative and positive. Clearly communicate goals, expectations, targets, and a new set of rules to be adhered to.

Let them know your employees what is required and expected of them. Keep them informed by giving them valuable information that makes them know how their job fits into the overall organization effort. Let's face the fact. All what employees really want is to get a face-to-face interaction time to time with both their managers and supervisors.

This communication makes them feel important and recognized. For you as a manager; You might have plenty of things to accomplish and attend to, and surely you might be competing with time.

However, a manager's major role is to assist your peers towards the achievement of organizational success. With this act, supervisors and managers can lead and magnify company success.

10. Ownership of Event

Give employees ownership of any event going to be organized by the company (inside or outside the company premises) to the employees who have some sort of experience of better handling of the events in the past.

Your employees will love to plan the event and is also encouraged. Moreover, if the event is planned & executed by the employees themselves, there are always no chances or fewer chances of any sort of complaint.

11. Diversity

Implement Diversity in the organization. Diversity is not limited to gender diversity only, but to take people from different cultures, set of beliefs, orientation, etc. Nowadays, Diversity is very important in any organization. People from different cultures have something different to bring to the board and which can improve employee engagement.

12. Retain them

Employees who are retired after attaining retirement age as per the policy defined in the company (most of the companies the retirement age 58 years or so), can be retained as a Consultant to support the business needs considering their vast experience which is fruitful to the organization. The employee feels encouraged and improves employee engagement.

13. Use promotional products

Promotional products are a great tool to help catch the attention of your organization at any job recruitment event. A custom gift is an effective way to exhibit your company's ideal work environment for aspiring candidates.

At job fairs, among the greatest challenges companies face is reaching out to passive applicants. Promotional gifts can definitely go a long way toward catching a candidate's attention and inviting them to consider your organization.

You need to make sure that your promotional gifts send the ideal message about your organization and the kind of employee you're searching for.

While promotional gifts such as logoed stainless steel mug or custom portfolio may create a good impression with a qualified job candidate, another reasonable way to grab the interest of job seekers is to replace your business cards with card magnets.

By placing your personal information on a customized magnet, your hiring job opportunity stands out from the crowd and shows applicants your organization's creative side.

14. Provide a Safe and Supportive Work Environment

When employees feel that they are in a safe and supportive work environment, they are going to be more open up and be willing to share new ideas and timely feedback.

Encourage your employees to speak directly to you as much as possible. Then, address their issues and problems by urgency and priority.

Convey the significance of building a socially sensitive workplace that leaves all workers feeling safe to work daily. Get all team leaders on board to facilitate correspondence and give a supportive work environment.

15. Favoritism

The results of employee Favoritism is very harmful in nature because the subsequent idea is inevitable Because of This, employees' Productivity, morale and connection with the manager will diminish thus creating disengaged workers which eventually leads to disengaged customers.

I advise you equally treat all workers and do away with favoritism at all costs.

Every employee wants a perception that each of them is being treated equivalently. Create a policy, and behavioral guidelines, strategies for requesting time off, and other work-related decisions you can consider.

16. Online Forum

Start an online forum that is available on the intranet site of the company where employees can post their issues related to work, work environment, HR Policies, Training needs, etc. Once in a month HR along with Departmental

Heads will have an open meeting with the employees (without mentioning the name of the employee) to resolve it then and there.

17. Open Court for discussion

An employee (at any level) can have a better understanding to solve the issue. There could be an open court of all employees where they discuss their issues and come up with the best solution to management.

By doing this, an employee will have the feeling that their views and thinking have importance in an organization.

8.9 Knowledge & Skills

1. Train the trainer

Send top-performing employees to a train-the-trainer class so they can help train new associates in their departments. Without incurring too much cost, this will help in knowledge transformation in the organizational employees.

2. Print Magazines

External print magazines

Games are not for everyone, so a lot of companies offer up to date magazines for their employees to peruse. This likewise helps the employee stay up to date with current affairs of the external world. Additionally, a fresh magazine goes excellent with a cup of coffee on a break.

In-house print magazines

Once in a couple of months or once in a quarter, these print magazines give a snapshot as to what is going in their organization which comprises sharing Company growth, Management Goals, Customer appreciations, Customer satisfaction, List of new customer sign-up, Sales review, Customer delivery and feedback, Partnership details, Upcoming projects, etc.

This is very important in large organizations to keep their people updated about happenings in the organization. Contributions from employees in the form of suggestions, good work, and articles can be added to the magazine.

3. Open To Speak

It enables employees to come up from speaking and stage fear. A group can be formed and weekly each member of the group to speak on a topic. Additionally, employees would learn some personal skills for him aimed at helping the organization for improved communication with their customers (internal/ external).

Are there consequences for speaking up? If employees fear that sharing their thoughts has the potential to come with professional, financial, social, physical, or emotional risks, then they are unlikely to share different perspectives or opinions. When employees know they're safe to share their thoughts (respectfully) without fear of punishment, it gives them a figurative green light. Foster a safe space for voices by paying attention to the way you react to feedback and ideas.

4. Job Rotation

With a job rotation mechanism, employees gain experience and skills by taking on new responsibilities of different departments, thus resulting in improved employee engagement. The company provides an opportunity for the Professionals to grow horizontally by rotating into different roles and to develop a Leadership pipeline by grooming fast track employees for Leadership positions for the future. Employees who have spent more than two-three years in a particular Department / Division/role could only be moved to another Department / Division/ role, where he/she should remain for a minimum of two years.

For a smooth takeover of the department, an overlapping period of minimum two-three months should be given to the executive. While rotating an employee, he/she will be extended all possible help to familiarize him with the new department/division, and necessary training inputs with respect to various key aspects like a commercial, technical, legal, etc. shall be arranged. Job Rotation will be done in the interrelated areas as per the Qualification/Command, Existing Competencies, and potential of the employees.

5. Sabbatical leaves

One year or 2 years, sabbatical leave for higher professional studies to employees once during the period of employment can be given. This will help the employees to pursue their full time higher education without fearing about the job.

6. Offer employees to attend a conference paid by the company

Offering company paid conferences & seminars to employees helps in getting knowledge about the happenings in the market like technological enhancements, new products, innovative tools, and techniques, etc. This will encourage learning in the employees, which will ultimately benefit the organization in the long run

7. Book Club

Form a book club in your organization on leadership, management, communications skills, or industry-related topics. The books are actually one of the best sources of information for years. One of the main reasons why books are considered as top sources of knowledge is because they provide unlimited facts to the readers. If you do the right set of research, you can probably find what you are looking for from books.

Also, Books are a permanent form of knowledge so that knowledge of past generations can be passed on to future generations.

8. Professional Membership

Start paying one professional membership per employee per year related to their job & Skills. It will help the employee to learn new tools, techniques, develop skill sets, aware of market trends about products & Services, etc. The learning is also beneficial to the company in the long run.

Here the important point is to provide the right set of membership, and there is no point in subscribing "Filmy magazine" for the employee working in the production line.

9. Support in Higher education

Support employees who are seeking higher professional qualifications. This will support in their career as well as the growth of the Company and to retain a strong technically qualified and result oriented workforce who can sustain the challenges in the fast-growing global market environment and look after the Company requirements. Some of the criteria or examples can be fixed in supporting the higher education are mentioned as follows, which can be referred to while making the Higher Education guidelines of the company:

- The employees who have completed at least two years of satisfactory and result oriented services with the Company with Exception/ High category('5' or '4' rating on a scale of 5) in Annual Performance appraisal and are ready to serve the Group in the years to come.

- Depending upon the budget of the Company, an employee can be sponsored 50%, 75% or 100% of the admission/tuition fees of the course.

- The employees who are having an excellent academic background, having sufficient working knowledge in their field, young, energetic and eager to acquire more profession/technical accuracy in their career, subject to the requirements of the company in the same domain can be given support for higher educational studies.

10. Internal Training

Having internal training classes once a month for employees in the organization to learn more about the company's products, services, leadership skills, communication skills, management skills, etc. Internal Trainers within the system can be originated to provide the training. This will also salvage some money that is needed for an external trainer.

11. Rotate person in leading a department meeting

Rotate each employee in the department leading his/her department meeting once in a while. It will aid the employees to overcome the fears and improve the skills in chairing the meetings.

12. Read Company News

Encourage employees to invest 10-15 minutes daily on reading company news and updates and become aware of what's going on in and about the company they were working in. Knowing close to their brand builds a sense of pride and belonging among the employees. They feel motivated to share ideas, hone new skills, and showcase their creative inclination. As a result, the employees stay inspired and continue to bring their best version to work.

13. Skill development Targets

Let employees plan their skill development targets for self, and we can help them achieve that with motivations, resources, training (on the job) or external paid training, etc. The targets can be to learn the tools and techniques required to perform a job in the work area, learning computers, learning a new language, improving communication skills, gain leadership skills, etc.

Once these targets are achieved with the help of an organization, the employee engagement, as well as the retention with the organization, will undoubtedly improve.

These activities promote knowledge, learning, and performance.

14. Leadership Development

While the Manager Controlled Development activities would help construct a high performing and engaged group. It's a Leadership Development activity which focuses on Sr. Level professionals concentrating on building up the administrative abilities for ensuring business coherence and continuing the development of the organization.

The activity includes helping Sr. Level professionals to prepare an Individual Development Plan for the year and implementation of the same by Coaching, instructing, tutoring, guiding, development, and so on.

15. Make Available Training Opportunities

The sense of worth an employee feels contributes to the company is at the core of employee engagement and serves as a base for retention.

Companies that offer training opportunities provide their employees with a feeling of stimulation and also increases the value of their organization too. This can play a factor in the internal marketing efforts mentioned earlier.

CHAPTER
Nine

*Evaluation of Employee
Engagement Strategy*

"Employees who believe that management is concerned about them as a whole person – not just an employee – are more productive, more satisfied, more fulfilled. Satisfied employees mean satisfied customers, which leads to profitability."

—Anne Mulcahy

So you have read all of the research, seen the benefits regarding improved productivity, innovation and commitment to company goals as well as the positive impact to the business organization's bottom line and are now ready to consider an employee engagement strategy.

How can you now determine what specific strategies and programs will increase employee engagement and what would make sense for your company to invest in?

Here are a few key criteria that employee engagement strategy should be evaluated against as you plan and develop effective programs for your company.

First, it is important to understand that there are many strategic initiatives that could influence employee engagement so the key to making the right decision will depend on your company's goals, budgets, and mission as well as the employee and leadership, demographics in your company.

1. **Assessment Survey**: Do you have an understanding of current engagement levels?

2. **Employee Interests:** Employee engagement must be considered through the employee's eyes, thoughts and feelings and cannot be mandated by corporate policy.

3. **ROI Considerations:** Employee engagement strategy and resulting programs should provide a strong return to the company. Some initiatives are easier to implement and measure than others.

4. **Managers Buy In:** Consideration must be given to how to get the support and buy-in of managers in your organization. They are such an important link in the employee engagement chain that a successful engagement strategy will need their support and participation or might otherwise fail or deliver inconsistent results.

No one strategy will fit all organizations, but these guidelines above can help you make decisions that are right for your organization.

CHAPTER
Ten

Measuring & Managing Employee Engagement

How to measure employee engagement?

There are a wide number of techniques in which employee engagement in any organization can be measured. The key techniques used are given here as under:-

1. Annual Surveys

2. Pulse surveys

3. One to one meetings

4. Exit Interviews

5. The productivity of the employee

6. Employee Turnover

Annual surveys are widely used across organizations.

Take action to improve employee engagement in the organization by acting upon the problem areas

Nothing is more discouraging to employees than to be asked for their feedback and see no action taken towards the resolution of their issues. Even the smallest actions taken to address concerns of the employee will let them know how their input is valued. Most importantly, when an employee feels valued will boost morale, motivate and encourage future input. So the point here is to listen to employee feedback and implement a definitive action plan on the problem areas.

One important reason why measuring employee engagement is so hard is because there's no real clear definition of what employee engagement is as it is defined by different organizations differently. Some organizations define it as happiness; some define it as satisfaction, some as a tool for retention of employees while others define it as a commitment to goals. The first step to improving something is to measure it.

Most companies that measure employee engagement completely fail to get the maximum return on their investment. They measure for the wrong reasons.

They don't fully integrate the measurement and management process into the broader management strategies of the business. They only measure half of what they should be measuring - and they don't do half the things they could do with the information they get.

Peter Drucker once famously said, "you can only manage what you measure." This statement is correct, of course, but it's also only reflective of half of the facts. In order to manage something, you do need to measure it. But, in order for the measurement to be worthwhile, you need to know what it is that you're measuring and why it is that you measure it.

Feedback Culture

The power of Feedback is spectacular. Building an incredible feedback culture at work can't solely bring terrific innovation and productivity; however, conjointly improves employee's motivation and engagement. However, it's easier to aforesaid than done. Human emotions, egos, hierarchies, and politics fester distrust among workers and forestall them from gap their minds. Fitting the correct examples from high leadership will play a polar role in building a dominant feedback culture. Samples of Feedback Cultures are:

Customer-focused

This is a culture wherever individuals have possession of their purchasers and are willing to chase away internally and argue on behalf of their customers. This can be a culture that adapts quickly to satisfy the wants of the marketplace as a result of they understand the desires and demands of the end-user.

Learning culture

This is a culture that encourages innovation, and wherever commitment is rewarded over loyalty. During this culture, innovation and acceptable risk-taking are rewarded, and folks are perpetually inspired not solely to learn, however, they apply their learning among the organization.

Ethical culture

This is a culture wherever individuals feel that the organization walks its speak. It's a culture that embraces real diversity and wherever individuals believe that they're a part of a larger smart which what they are doing makes a distinction. During this culture, individuals are engaged and authorized.

I had met with one of my friends, who have started these activities 4 -5 years ago in his organization. They have been playing games, making the environment lite with some random topic discussions, celebrating people birthdays, recognizing the employees for their good work, sip a tea together, play communication-related games, going out on a picnic, taking care of health and well being, celebrating festivals together as well.

He has witnessed a huge difference in productivity and employee's willingness towards work and reduced employee turnover by this.

CHAPTER
Eleven

*Start Employee Engagement
in Short Time*

There are many ways in which one can incorporate an Employee Engagement Strategy within your own business or organization, but for the purposes of this chapter, I am going to focus on what I believe are the main ways in which you can start to do this effectively and in as short a time-frame as possible.

If you can actively incorporate an Employee Engagement strategy into your own organization and develop these practices, you should start to see results within a few months. I would recommend you find an easy way to measure these results that not only works for you but is not too time-consuming.

It should be something relatively simple, such as carrying out a customer service survey, measuring client levels before the Employee Engagement strategy was implemented and afterward, or carrying out a staff survey about six months after you start using engagement tools within the organization to measure morale and staff satisfaction.

Although, when an Employee Engagement strategy is used correctly, you should start to see physical results, such as productivity increases, absenteeism decreasing and improved retention rates.

Employee Engagement does not require any direct financial investment, unless you decide to invest in staff training, for example; the commitment you are making to your staff is one of the time.

Dedicating time to engaging with your employees and assessing their own engagement levels within your company is an investment, which will pay dividends later on, but in order for this to work, you must make the commitment, to begin with.

Develop Your Leadership Skills

In order to promote Employee Engagement within your organization, it goes without saying that you need to demonstrate superb leadership skills. Your employees must see you as someone who is supportive, understanding and credible.

You should focus on demonstrating your ability to listen to your employees and be willing to take on board their comments and suggestions. One can do this is by holding regular staff engagement sessions.

This can be done either on a one-to-one basis or as Town Hall meeting, which is an information session usually used to update your employees and during which an open forum is actively encouraged and promoted.

Depending on the size & volume of your organization, you may opt for a one-to-one session with each employee. Focus on listening rather than speaking and try to encourage an open discussion. Promote the ethos within your company that your "door is always open" and try to make time for your employees.

Learn to Monitor Your Employee Behavior Effectively

An engaged and satisfied employee will do a number of things which are both measurable and identifiable. If your employees are emotionally and intellectually committed to your organization, they will consistently say positive things about the company, their department and their co-workers in both internal and external environments. Not only will they work harder, but they will do it cheerfully and without being asked to.

They will strive to achieve both their personal and professional best and will remain committed to achieving high productivity levels and, if they work in a customer-led environment, they will strive to not only retain existing customers but work hard to win more. Engaged employees will stay within the organization they work in and will remain committed to doing so.

It is not difficult to tell an engaged employee from a disengaged one - the secret is what you do with the information you are presented with. Do you actively strive to improve things by listening to what your employees are telling you (remember that behavior is not always about what you hear and see, but equally what you don't hear and don't see)?

Showing up late for work, slovenly behavior, moaning and complaining are all very obvious signs of employee disengagement, but you must also watch for signs of discontentment in other ways - absenteeism through constant and unexplained illness, a usually outgoing employee becoming quiet and uncommunicative, issues with co-workers or complaints received directly from customers are all signs of an employee who is fast becoming disengaged.

If you can incorporate an Employee Engagement Strategy into your workplace, you will be amazed at how simple and easily you can improve productivity and reduce problems.

It is my belief that an engaged and committed workforce means better customer satisfaction levels and a more profitable organization, so actively using Employee Engagement within your own business can only mean good things for you and for your company.

CHAPTER
Twelve

Carry Out a Staff Survey

Sometimes carrying out a survey among staff can be a real eye-opener, so be prepared to face some truths you didn't want to face before! Remember - if you are going to embrace Employee Engagement, it's all or nothing - no half measures, unfortunately, otherwise it simply won't work.

It is also important to address the area of how your employees relate to and engage with one another.

There may be internal issues within your organization of which you are unaware, so to adequately assess the results of your survey in order to measure current staff engagement levels, you will need to make sure you include questions on your survey which relate to "Management", "Co-Workers" or "Peers" and how your employees view others.

This is important, as it will give you a picture of how each section of your company relates to each other. For example, you may receive comments from staff members who criticize other areas of the company, such as the IT Department or the HR Department.

Be prepared to hear comments such as "IT never answer the phones when I call" or "HR treat me like I am just a number." You might also see answers such as,

"Management doesn't even know who I am" or "I've never seen the MD, I know where her office is, but he/she has never spoken to me... "

While it is difficult as an employer or business owner to hear and read these comments, it is vital that you take on board how your employees view the culture within the organization.

If your company promotes an ethos whereby employees feel they are listened to, understood and cared about, recognized and trained in the skill sets they will want to stay in the company and will not seek employment elsewhere.

The benefit of this is that you retain their talent, expertise and experience. Imagine losing your best employee to a rival company because he/she is not accepted by your organization and you didn't listen to him or her!

They've spent 5 or 6 years building up their career in your company, bringing in new clients, developing themselves, satisfied customers at times and becoming so good that, when the time is right, another organization comes along and snaps them up, all because you didn't have time to listen to what employee was trying to tell you.

A word of caution... once you gather the data you need you must be prepared to act on the feedback you receive, otherwise the exercise is pointless and a waste of time (and, possibly, money if you engage the services of a professional survey company to assist you - and if you do, you must ensure they are experienced in dealing with staff and phrasing questions sensitively and appropriately).

You must be prepared to really examine what is driving disengagement within your organization and then take the appropriate steps to remedy this.

Once you are armed with your survey results, you will immediately know the areas you need to focus on. While it may not be financially practical or possible to give everyone a pay rise or bonus, try to think of other ways in which you can compensate your staff for the work they do.

The Gallup Organization began creating a widely accepted feedback system for organizations that would identify and measure elements of employee engagement mostly linked to the bottom line--things such as sales growth, increased share price in the stock market, productivity and customer loyalty.

After hundreds of focus groups and thousands of interviews with employees in a variety of industries, Gallup came up with the Q12, a 12-question survey that identifies strong feelings of employee engagement. Results from the survey show a strong correlation between high scores and superior job performance. Here are those 12 questions:

a. Do you know what is expected of you at work?

b. Do you have the materials and equipment you need to do your work right?

c. At work, do you have the opportunity to do what you do best every day?

d. In the last seven days, have you received recognition or praise for doing good work?

e. Does your supervisor, or someone at work, seem to care about you as a person?

f. Is there someone at work who encourages your development?

g. At work, do your opinions seem to count?

h. Does the mission/purpose of your company make you feel your job is important?

i. Are your associates (fellow employees) committed to doing quality work?

j. Do you have a best friend at work?

k. In the last six months, has someone at work talked to you about your progress?

l. During the last year, have you had opportunities at work to learn and grow?

CHAPTER
Thirteen

Measuring The Return on Investment of Employee Engagement

Employee engagement programs, despite the fact that not an enormous cost, has been an obvious objective to trim as they frequently need following explicit measurements and are difficult to quantify as far as Return on Investment (ROI) and Value on Investment (VOI).

Measuring (and then consequently increasing) your ROI and VOI of employee engagement projects can be accomplished when the best possible measurements are set up and all the more so when attached to quantifiable business drivers or results.

Some of the examples of the business result are given here as under:-

1. *Reduced Employee Turnover i.e., the Attrition rate*

2. *Improved Customer Satisfaction*

3. *More customer acquisitions*

4. *Technological Advancements in the organization*

5. *Increase in the price of shares of the company in the stock market*

The ROI and VOI accessible to organizations will truly rely upon what sort of program is executed and what the objectives are for the program. For instance, a program to improve teamwork and communication will have an altogether different ROI than an incentive plan for meeting the operational demands of high production targets of the festival.

As with any investment, it is important to be able to measure. Secondly, if the investment proves to be worthwhile, it makes good sense to increase that investment to the maximum point just shy of diminishing returns.

Although some companies who do invest in incentive plans or other motivational strategies still underutilize them; the programs are marginalized as 'feel-good' exercises. Others - the better business leaders who understand the value of employee engagement programs- see things a lot differently.

Exercise before you go ahead..!!

Where can your company expect to see benefits and returns from your investments in engagement programs? What types of benefits are achievable and measurable? Can you translate the metrics into financial terms?

CHAPTER
Fourteen

Barriers to Employee Engagement

From my experience of working with people in organizations over the years, I have observed that the people who are the most engaged are those whose values fit with those of the organization, the people they work with and the work they are doing.

The most engaged are also those who have found their own personal meaning in their work and who feel in synch with the organization's goals.

One of the most challenging tasks for keeping people engaged lies with the leadership of the organizations beginning with their immediate supervisor upwards. Research has shown that almost 50 to 60% of the employees are disengaged and out of that, about 10 to 20% are actively disengaged. You know what actively disengaged people can do, don't you. They could destroy, everything you are working for and trying to create in terms of, a healthy work environment.

The seven main barriers to employee engagement activities are listed below:

1. Management Approach

Management Approach towards the employee Engagement programs is not the convincing one or not on the priority. Although they make decisions in the organization, but then change their minds quickly, and not always for apparent reasons.

2. Operational Demands

In meeting the operational demands of customers, not enough time or focus on employee engagement activities. Gravity is to fulfill the demands of external customers.

3. Budget Issues

The budget of the organization is very limited. It is either due to the profitability of the organization or less budget allocated to employee engagement activities.

4. Generic assumptions by the engagement leaders

Engagement leaders assume it as generic, i.e., and they assume that all people are engaged by the same factors (namely the factors listed in their engagement survey). It is undoubtedly true that there are some common factors that help keep most people engaged, like having a decent salary, caring supervisor, etc. However, we are all individuals, and so all of us are engaged by different things.

5. The judgment of External & internal factors

Most organizations don't take account of whether their employees are primarily driven by external factors or internal ones. A key determinant of the extent to which a person is engaged is whether they have an internal locus of control i.e., they believe that they can influence and control their world and what happens to them, or whether they have an external locus of control, i.e., they believe that other people or things determine what happens to them.

I would argue that people with an internal locus of control are more consistently engaged than people with an external locus of control. This is significant to a company when deciding what they need to do to increase their engagement levels.

6. Failure in engagement Survey

The Employee engagement survey must consist of a set question directed towards the needs of organization culture. Failing to ask the right set of questions or interpreting the survey outcomes will result in a barrier to employee engagement in the organization. Measurement frequently takes precedence over execution when it comes to engagement. However, you need to first get an insight into the people you're trying to engage.

7. Competency of Engagement Leader

If Engagement leader does not possess the competencies required (Decision Maker, Passionate, Active, caring, etc.) for implementing the employee engagement programs, the purpose will be failed drastically.

CHAPTER
Fifteen

Main Flaws in Organizations Approach Engagement

Over the years, I've learned that employees that are most engaged are those whose values fit with that of their organization, the folks they work with, and the job they are doing. The most engaged ones are also people who have discovered their own personal relevance and meaning in their job and who feel in synch with all the company's goals.

Measurement is significant, but only if you understand what to quantify and if it gives you the ability to know what's working and what you need to do otherwise. I know some companies that have completed employee engagement surveys and scored highly, whereas however, moral engagement is extremely low. This connotes that they are not measuring the right things and/or they aren't taking actions that produce a difference.

It may certainly be challenging to navigate your way towards creating an effective employee engagement approach.

If you go through all the research and literature, it is easy to get overwhelmed and confused about where to start.

First and foremost, you need to decide your point of focus. What does engagement mean to you personally? As soon as you have a definition that is appropriate for you, it will be a lot easier to decide what you want to do and change.

I so much believe in Simplicity and when I talk to organizations people, I do start with asking these basic questions:

- **What is meant by engagement?**
- **Why do you wish to increase your engagement?**
- **How engaged are you now?**
- **What changes would you need to see in people's behavior, emotions and understanding?**

It's also useful to consider three basic ways that individuals get engaged

Emotional: You need to access how people feel about their job, associations, managers, etc.. People are emotional beings and the most hardened business people must definitely feel something about what they're doing to be truly engaged with it.

Behavioral: What exactly do folks do or Intend to do later on? For instance, do they want to stay in business, do they put the utmost effort into the job they can, do they recommend the company to other prospective employees and clients?

Intellectual: Do people support and believe in the company's goals or their part of the company

Measurement frequently takes precedence over execution when it comes to engagement. However, you need first to get an insight into the people you're trying to engage in.

Of course, the results are embedded within the implementation, and you can also make the insight gathering part of this implementation rather than rendering it sequential. This is a very attractive and economical approach, especially in the present economic climate.

It's not essential to start with a questionnaire even in the event that you have thousands of employees!

The following will be absolute principles:

1. Helping managers to know and understand

    a. What engages them (being Engaged is contagious and it is challenging to get people engaged if their managers aren't engaged!)

    b. How to be an engaging supervisor

2. Assisting your people to gain insight into, what engages them and what their job means to them. Have them discuss this insight with their fellow managers.

3. Communicating well with your people about matters of significance to them.

These are the principles and the foundation for any engagement program. Starting with these points keeps things easy and cost-effective and providing you the best chance of raising engagement levels quickly within the organization.

CHAPTER
Sixteen

Future of Employee Engagement

"The next 15 years of employee engagement will no longer be an HR-initiative, but critical responsibility of your managers. Bots, smart alerts, and predictive analytics will support managers in enabling their teams to be most effective."

—Megan Maslanka
Director of Client Success

Employee engagement isn't an overnight resolution; moreover, it's a strategic organization decided to adopt a cultural matrix to recruit, engage and retain the best employees in the organization. In the next 10-15 years or so, employee engagement will take the employee/employer relationship to the next level.

Half the struggle is won if managers can operate with a mindset that employees are immortal customers too. Just like customer-focused organizations know how to attract customers, engage to keep them happy, and manage angry customers, the HR team needs to take a standardized guide to handle employees as well.

Increase the feeling of individual control within everyday work. Engagement is an individual choice, and choice implies having control of at least some daily decisions.

As a leader, the more you can enable your employees to make decisions relevant to their work, AND increase their confidence in making a good decision, the more likely it is they CAN and WILL engage.

We have plenty of reward programs. We closely watch people who contribute towards product quality, process quality, internal trainers who train colleagues, people who bring best practices from outside and implement if here and so on. They are rewarded and as you know, the rewards are inspiring and infectious. Moreover,

1. **Employee Engagement will be more authentic and real**

2. **Organizations focus on Employee Engagement and engagement level will increase across the globe**

3. **Organizations will understand the value of engagement and conduct their surveys to understand employee-driven engagement strategies.**

The bottom line is that employee engagement works good in any organization, assuming that it's implemented in the right spirits. With these tips, employee's satisfaction increases and surely enough the satisfied employees produce more and remain in their jobs longer.

I hope that this book would prove to be a simple guide for Employee engagement.

Conclusion

Employee engagement is highly crucial to the success of any organization. Engaged employees are committed, motivated and entirely devoted to their work. They strive to perform their best as a devoted employee and they concentrate on making the company they work for a greater and better place to work.

They see the "bigger picture" and understand the role they play in furthering the company's mission and vision. They're not just satisfied - they're motivated, committed, appreciated and empowered.

Unfortunately, engaged employees are the minority. Employees who aren't engaged bring down the morale of other employees. Plus, disengaged employees are less productive and are more likely to seek alternative employment.

Most employees deal with continuous-time restraints. Between working, dealing with young kids and perhaps aging parents, it leaves little or no time for them to concentrate on their own wellbeing and health. They might not consume a balanced diet and fail to find sufficient time for exercise, and of course, suffered from stress and anxiety.

These factors make it hard for them to be engaged in their work in the organization. Employers can help by emphasizing health & well-being at the workplace. A healthy employee has more resources to be engaged and is likely to be more productive too for the organization.

If you want better employee engagement, make sure your employees stay healthy, their work should be appreciated and recognized, efforts should be made for collaboration and alignment with the organization. Moreover, his personal & work skills need to be improved. When you focus on these points, employees know you care about them, and that motivates them to go the "extra mile."

Employee engagement is critical to your company reducing its business costs and improving team morale.

Hope, The book offered you Employee Engagement Practices and activities that an organization needs to improve employee satisfaction and engagement.

START TODAY!

Exercise

What best 10 activities/practices you like the most... and sooner or later will implement in your organization?

____

____

____

____

____

____

____

____

____

____

____

____

____

References

Albercht, S. L., Bakker, A. B., Gruman, J. A., Macey, W. H., & Saks, A. M. (2015). Employee engagement, human resource management practices and competitive advantage: An integrated approach.Journal of Organizational Effectiveness: People and Performance, 2, 7–35.

Andrew, O. C., & Sofian, S. (2012). Individual factors and work outcomes of employee engagement. Procedia: Social and Behavioral Sciences, 40, 498–508.

Anitha, J. (2014). Determinants of employee engagement and their impact on employee performance. International Journal of Productivity and Performance Management, 63, 308–323.

Berens, R. (2013). The roots of employee engagement: A strategic approach.Employment Relations Today, 40, 43–49.

Gallup (2006).'Engaged employees inspire company innovation', Gallup Management Journal,

Kompaso, S. M., & Sridevi, M. S. (2010). Employee engagement: The key to improving performance. International Journal of Business and Management, 5, 89–98.

Kahn, W.A. (1990). 'Psychological conditions of personal engagement and disengagement at work', Academy of Management Journal

Macey, W.H. & Schneider, B. (2008). 'The meaning of employee engagement', International and Organizational Psychology: Perspectives in Science and Practice

Menguc, B., Auh, S., Fisher, M., & Haddad, A. (2013). To be engaged or not to be engaged: The antecedents and consequences of service employee engagement.Journal of Business Research

Mishra, K., Boynton, L., & Mishra, A. (2014). Driving employee engagement: The expanded role of internal communications. International Journal of Business Communications, 51, 183–202.

Swarnalatha, C., & Prasanna, T. S. (2013). Employee engagement and line of sight.International Journal of Research in Business Management, 1, 1–8.

Saks, A. M. (2006). 'Antecedents and consequences of employee engagement', Journal of Managerial Psychology, 21(7): 600–19

SHRM (2008) White Paper: Employee Engagement and Organizational Performance: How do you know your employees are engaged?

www.shrm.org/hrresources/whitepapers_published/CMS_012127.asp.

Vance, R. (2006a). Employee Engagement and Commitment. Alexandr ia, VA: SHRM.

Vance, R.J. (2006b).'Employee engagement and commitment: A guide to understanding, measuring and increasing engagement in your organization', Society for Human Resource Management, 1–45.

https://www.vocoli.com/media/3099/managers-guide-employee-engagement.pdf

https://www.infectioncontroltoday.com/hand-hygiene/study-reveals-correlation-between-handwashing-and-employee-engagement

https://www.getfeedback.net/kb/12-questions-to-measure-employee-engagement

https://www.shrm.org/hr-today/news/hr-magazine/Pages/0510fox3.aspx

https://www.cos-mag.com/safety-leadership-culture/31349-measuring-the-roi-and-voi-of-employee-engagement/~/safety-awards/readers-choice-awards/

https://ezinearticles.com/?Employee-Engagement:-Six-Causes-of-Disengaged-Employees&id=7057332

https://www.slideshare.net/vicnagda/employee-engagement-activities-28103676

http://shodhganga.inflibnet.ac.in/bitstream/10603/174076/7/07_chapter%202.pdf